GREAT WRITERS KURT VONNEGUT

GREAT WRITERS

KURT VONNEGUT

John Tomedi

Foreword by Peter J. Reed

CHELSEA HOUSE
PUBLISHERS
A Haights Cross Communications ⚫ Company
Philadelphia

CHELSEA HOUSE PUBLISHERS

VP, NEW PRODUCT DEVELOPMENT Sally Cheney
DIRECTOR OF PRODUCTION Kim Shinners
CREATIVE MANAGER Takeshi Takahashi
MANUFACTURING MANAGER Diann Grasse

Staff for KURT VONNEGUT

EXECUTIVE EDITOR: Matt Uhler
ASSOCIATE EDITOR: Susan Naab
EDITORIAL ASSISTANT: Sharon Slaughter
PRODUCTION EDITOR: Megan Emery
SERIES AND COVER DESIGNER: Takeshi Takahashi
COVER: Christopher Felver/CORBIS
LAYOUT: EJB Publishing Services

A Haights Cross Communications Company

http://www.chelseahouse.com

First Printing

9 8 7 6 5 4 3 2 1

Library of Congress Cataloging-in-Publication Data

Tomedi, John.
    Kurt Vonnegut / John Tomedi.
      p. cm. — (Great writers)
    Includes bibliographical references (p.   ).
    ISBN 0-7910-7848-5
    1. Vonnegut, Kurt—Criticism and interpretation. I. Title. II. Series:
Great writers (Philadelphia, Pa.)

  PS3572.O5Z865 2004
  813'.54—dc22
                                        2004006274

TABLE OF CONTENTS

*I have become an enthusiast of the printed word
again. I have to be that, I now understand, because
I want to be a character in all of my works.*
      —Kurt Vonnegut, *Between Time and Timbuktu,* xv

IN CHAPTER 5 OF THIS Critical biography, John Tomedi quotes
Kurt Vonnegut's saying the above after his venture into playwriting
with "Happy Birthday, Wanda June." Plays, Vonnegut found, left
him no role, except that of the puppeteer behind the scenes, pulling
the strings. But increasingly throughout the novels that had
preceded the play, Vonnegut had brought himself into his fiction,
exemplified in *Slaughterhouse-Five*'s "That was me. I was there."

The extraordinary degree to which Vonnegut invests himself in
his fiction makes the biographical approach John Tomedi takes in
the present work most appropriate. The linkages between the life
and the writing are ever-present in the novels of Kurt Vonnegut. It
is not unusual for writers to draw on or adapt personal experiences
in their work, or to fictionalize as characters people they have met.
Likewise, other writers use a first person narrator, an "I," who
takes a point of view that may be close to the author's own.
Vonnegut transcends both of these influences of biography upon
content and narration. Tomedi explores the evolution of this
distinctive quality as he traces the years and the pages of Kurt
Vonnegut's long career.

And what a long career that has been. As Tomedi points out,
even half a century after the publication of Vonnegut's first novel,

Player Piano, all of his books are still in press. (The short story collection *Canary in a Cathouse* was effectively subsumed into *Welcome to the Monkey House*.) Such longevity is rare, and only comes about when successive generations of readers find the works still relevant and satisfying. That acceptance is perhaps more remarkable than that Vonnegut has remained productive and imaginatively fertile over more than fifty years, constantly experimenting and evolving.

In recounting Vonnegut's life, John Tomedi shows how as a child he found that he could get the attention of parents and older siblings by being funny, telling little jokes. Years later Vonnegut would describe his novels as mosaics made up of tiles, each tile being a joke. In high school and college Vonnegut wrote for student newspapers and learned the direct, clipped style that came to characterize his fiction. The Great Depression following the 1929 stock market crash left a deep impression. His unemployed father shrank into himself feeling a loss of self esteem, while his mother became increasingly desperate as her lifestyle declined, finally committing suicide. These events helped shape Vonnegut's social, political and economic views. He probes the question of "what are people for?" What gives them a sense of worth, and what answers their loneliness and alienation? Noting the fragmenting of the extended family of his childhood, he stresses the need for community and mutual support.

Most dramatic is his surviving the apocalyptic firebombing of Dresden while a prisoner of war in 1945. Witnessing the destruction of the city and the deaths of so many of its people amplifies his pre-existing pacifist instincts. He sees what perverted science can do to humanity and, confronted by the corpses of so many innocent civilian victims of the "good guys" of the war, comes to view Dresden as the emblem of the terrible moral ambiguities societies must face. His postwar work as a public relations "flack" influences his view of the impact of the corporate system on the lives of average Americans, and leads to searching explorations of the ethics of the writer who, be it in PR or novels, makes up beguiling fictions. Thus all of these events come to shape his writing.

Tomedi several times makes mention of Vonnegut's being an atheist, or, as he himself puts it, an inheritor of the family tradition of being "German free thinkers." That, by the way, is not to say that Vonnegut dismisses Christianity. Tomedi quotes his saying, "I admire Christianity more that anything—Christianity as symbolized by gentle people sharing a common bowl." While he several times satirizes the behavior of fundamentalist sects (and other religions), Vonnegut cites the Sermon on the Mount and others of Jesus's teachings as models for living with consideration for others, especially the deprived. But his view of existence as contingent, random, not guided by some divine purpose, influences not just content but form. No doubt Vonnegut's *personal* experiences reinforce his view of a random or Absurd universe. The bewildering succession of events he has experienced—the Ardennes battle, the Dresden immolation, his mother's suicide, the near-simultaneous deaths of his sister Alice and her husband John Adams—must have given personally-felt substance to a philosophical belief. And so postmodernism, with its underlying assumption that meaning is constructed out of language, becomes his natural medium. As Tomedi recounts, *Cat's Cradle*, with its made-up San Lorenzon dialect, made-up Bokononist religion, and its toyshop model-railway-layout geography, marks the point where Vonnegut's postmodernism becomes most apparent.

That Vonnegut has outlasted many of his contemporaries does not mean that his career has been without controversy. As Tomedi shows, he has been subject to attack both by those who would censor him and by assorted critics. His would-be censors, mostly fundamentalist Christian conservatives, have objected to his diction and his socio-religious views. The relatively few four letter words occur mostly in situations where the characters probably would in reality use them, although elsewhere (*Breakfast of Champions*) he seeks to dispel the pious inhibitions that have adhered to what are, after all, just words. As a "free thinker" and an anthropologist, Vonnegut has irreverently satirized our need for and creation of religions (most conspicuously in *Cat's Cradle*), evoking further ire in some quarters. As to the critics, Tomedi balances his account by citing both press reviewers and academics who, by and large, suspect that Vonnegut is too facile, too easily banished to the realms of popular fiction, to be taken very seriously.

Vonnegut has famously noted that his earliest critics sought to cast him as a science fiction writer, and that the label has tended to stick. This began with his first short story, "Report on the Barnhouse Effect," and such titles as *Utopia 14* (the Bantam reissued *Player Piano*) and *The Sirens of Titan* encouraged its continuance. Vonnegut points out that his early works were written while he worked at the General Electric research laboratories, so reflected the world he saw every day. Beyond that, as Tomedi with the support of others demonstrates, Vonnegut simply makes use of science fiction plots and devices toward a more profound end. The science fiction is never the *point*. Vonnegut clearly has been successful in making the modes of popular fiction a way to address serious issues, both topical and timeless. Consequently, he has so engaged his audiences that his books remain in print and he remains in demand as a speaker. *Hocus Pocus* is as relevant to the early twenty-first century as *Player Piano* was to the 1950's.

The other source of Vonnegut's enduring popularity is, of course, that he is funny. Discussing a writer's humor often comes across rather like explaining a joke—nothing funny remains. In this book, Tomedi mentions Vonnegut's admiration of the radio comedians of the Depression years, and how he appreciated their sense of timing. Certainly one sees that in Vonnegut's speaking engagements, the "How to Get a Job Like Mine" performances, which evince more than a touch of stand-up comedy. Such timing is harder to get into writing, but he frequently manages it. There are short, punchy one-joke segments, or longer lead-ups to a brisk punch line, or shaggy-dog endings that lead into a space that we fill with a groan. Much of his humor depends on disparity, often between the painful and the seemingly glib. *Slaughterhouse-Five* provides the most obvious example, with "So it goes," following every death. That often seems laughable, such as when it occurs after a discussion of whether the novel is dead. But as the carnage mounts, reaching into its contemporary audience's pain at the murders of Martin Luther King and Robert F. Kennedy, "So it goes" becomes an incremental refrain that takes on added meaning with its insistent, deadly repetition.

Vonnegut also finds humor in the disparities between our expectations or aspirations and the realities that life deals us. His plots are replete with things that "shouldn't happen," that are unexpected or illogical. These range from the celebratory pantomime staged by the British prisoners of war for the dazed American arrivals in *Slaughterhouse-Five,* to the dreadful accident of *Deadeye Dick's* Rudy Waltz firing aimlessly over the rooftops and killing a woman, earning him the ludicrous title of "Deadeye Dick." Vonnegut's more bizarre inventions amplify such disparities and their sometimes comic effects. The variable gravity in *Slapstick* transforms something we take for granted as unchanging. While it wreaks terrible havoc, it also, in its lighter moments, makes us laugh, as people toss manhole covers like frisbies and all the men get erections. Sometimes the painful comedy involves characters who are "crazy as a bedbug," but Vonnegut's humor often involves decent people trying to cope with an irrational world. He describes this best in the Prologue of *Slapstick,* seeing life as a series of tests of his "limited agility and intelligence."

> The fundamental joke with Laurel and Hardy, it seems to me, was that they did their best with every test. They never failed to bargain in good faith with their destinies, and were screamingly adorable and funny on that account. (*Slapstick* 1)

So in the midst of his description of the worst human tragedy he has witnessed, Vonnegut makes his stand-in Billy Pilgrim a hobbling scarecrow, bemusedly smiling at the children who mock him.

Such humor may be born of a pessimistic view of human success in dealing with an Absurd universe, and Tomedi in this book draws much attention to Vonnegut's pessimism. Yet this kind of humor, rather like the "gallows humor" that prevailed in the trenches of World War I, can help sustain in adversity. It is also a kind of humor that implies compassion and warmth, as we see in the Laurel and Hardy quotation above, and if there is one value that pervades Vonnegut's writing it is the treatment of others with kindness, decency and respect. "Goddam it, you've got to be kind," Eliot Rosewater says, and there, crudely summed up, is the essence of Vonnegut. He does, after all, provide triumphs in the face of the world he views so darkly. In *Slapstick*, one person after another helps Melody accomplish her unlikely journey to find her grandfather, and the cynical boy Chrono of *The Sirens of Titan* finally cries, "Thank you, Mother and Father, for the gift of life!" There may be no happy endings, but there are encouraging moments of people helping people, acts of kindness and decency, posed in the face of incoherence and catastrophe.

As we have seen, Vonnegut's own life has been dogged by tragedy. His admired father's painful withdrawal. His mother's suicide. The shocking death of his brother-in-law John Adams, hours before the cancer-caused death of his beloved sister Alice. Capture and imprisonment in the Second World War. Surviving the Dresden fire-raid and being put to work exhuming corpses from the wreckage. Divorce, and his first wife's death from cancer. His own struggles with depression, his failed suicide in 1984, and his near death in a house fire in 2000. It would all seem much to bear. Yet here he is, at eighty-one still a delightfully funny man, still working, still with his message of peace and decency, still resilient. Here he is.

Peter J. Reed
March 2004

CHAPTER ONE

Out of Indianapolis

I'm no brighter or better educated than anyone else,
but it seems to me we're in terrible danger. I see no
reason that would persuade me we'll escape a third
world war. I see a number of reasons to conclude
we're on a collision course with ecological disaster.
On a less spectacular note, I think we can be
absolutely certain a nuclear plant is going to blow
within the next few years; the mathematical odds of
that are intolerable.

—Kurt Vonnegut, *Conversations with Kurt Vonnegut*

HOW A HAPLESS JOKESTER like Kurt Vonnegut rose to become
nothing short of a guru to millions in the 1960's and 1970's,
gaining uncanny critical attention while still in his prime, drawing
the ire of literary and social traditionalists, and earning his place as
an American cultural mainstay may very well be the subject of one
of his own books. This is the irony in Vonnegut's work: the plain
absurdity in his fiction is the stuff of his life. In a bizarre,
Vonnegutian twist, the new style of fiction he spearheaded—one
that acknowledged fiction as a fiction, a falsehood; one that
proffered strong dialectics out of altogether absurd environments;

one that paired ever-present humor with grim, pessimistic outlooks—developed from his conventional start in the mainstream pages of the *Saturday Evening Post, Collier's*, and other magazines, and his heavy messages first appeared under the cover of cheap drugstore paperbacks. The irony ends, though, with the admission that Kurt Vonnegut is, of course, entirely conscious of all of this: his universe of chance outcomes and dubious heroes is precisely the experience of his life.

Vonnegut is ensconced in the century that produced him. Through war and genocide, through amazing and unchecked technological advancement, through the Atomic age and its threat of global annihilation, through the exercise of democracy when the civil rights movement and protestors of the Vietnam war needed democracy the most, Vonnegut the satirist emerged a stalwart pacifist in the face of ever-increasing armament, a neo-Luddite during the most dramatic period of invention in human history, and a prolific atheist under multiple fundamentalist movements. He wrote himself into the middle of things, taking pains to circumscribe the events of the last century with purpose, humor, and accessibility in mind. He effervesced to roil the American optimism and apathy of the post-World War II era, operating under the notion that art should be held responsible for social critique.

Slaughterhouse-Five (1969) launched the author into the national consciousness, finding its place on banned-books and best-seller lists alike. In actuality, it was a culmination of the sort of fiction he had been writing for twenty years, though it was received as a timely and groundbreaking masterwork, something new for the American readership to experience. But *Slaughterhouse-Five*'s real power was in its embrace by a combustible college audience second-guessing American efforts in Vietnam. Vonnegut's exoneration of pacifism and his easy lampoons of accepted belief systems emboldened a generation against authority and placed him quickly on the syllabi of literature courses. He found himself in the late sixties and early seventies enjoying the role of advocate, public-spokesman, activist. For almost a decade in the 1960's and 1970's, Vonnegut's work and words gained an almost religious reverence in the eyes of his younger readers. But along with this popularity, the seeming simplicity of his prose and presentation put the author under the heavy shrewdness of the Academy and the literary establishment, and his iconoclasm brought on renewed cries for censorship. Thus, for his calls for change he was hailed as the spokesperson of a progressive generation; for his experimental narratives, he was tagged corrupter of literature, and for a few four-letter words, a corrupter of youth.

This is not to say that even in the present time Kurt Vonnegut is lacking in popular stamina. In 2004 his twenty-one books, which include fourteen novels, three non-fiction titles featuring essays and autobiographical material, two collections of short stories, a libretto of pretended interviews, and a play, are all in print. Four of his works have been made into feature films. Adding to this his years on the lecture circuit and his countless interviews and essays for newspapers and magazines, Kurt Vonnegut is the model of modern literary fame.

Vonnegut's tendencies are not difficult to spot. Jokes proliferate in his writing. Short chapters, paragraphs, and sentences make for an often easy read, and many of his novels might be had in one sitting. For all the humor and simplicity, however, his examinations of the human condition produce a view that is often pessimistic. Beginning with *Player Piano* (1952), Vonnegut explores the effects of the increased mechanization of society, especially as it displaces human beings from meaningful work and, therefore, meaningful existence. The same loss of dignity is portrayed in *God Bless You, Mr. Rosewater* (1965), where money and material objects dictate the lives of so many, and simple decency toward one another is possible only at the edge of insanity. *The Sirens of Titan* (1959), *Cat's Cradle* (1963), *Slaughterhouse-Five*, and others sketch the futility of existence, the failure of religion and technology to improve the human condition, and the place of chance and misfortune in life. War and cataclysm seem always ready to take root and destroy. Loneliness is endemic, becoming a major theme in *Slapstick* (1976) and the works following. Suicide is everywhere.

His willingness to question humanity's relationship to time and technology had Vonnegut dubbed a science fiction writer early in his career, though to dwell on the presence of aliens and futuristic settings in some of his works is to ignore much of what he says and how he says it. His frequent lampoons of societal ills make him a literary descendant of Jonathan Swift, and he writes arguably the funniest prose since Mark Twain. His experimentation with narrative style, with metafictional forms, with ideas of truth and fiction, align him with postmodernists like Pynchon and Rushdie, Heller and Reed, a pack of writers saying things differently than English departments were teaching, who, moreover, denied that a grave message precluded the possibility of humor. But Vonnegut breaks away from these in his racing, simple style and diction. Reading a Vonnegut book is hardly a chore. If the author has a theory of literature, it is a resistance to the notion that good writing has to be difficult to understand.

For all his synonymity with innovation, Kurt Vonnegut grew up in the Middle America of Depression-era Indianapolis. The views, settings, and situations his novels portray find much of their source in his experiences growing up—his ancestry, family life, and service in World War II—the details of which Vonnegut has been happy to impart.

Kurt Vonnegut, Jr., was born November 11, 1922, the youngest of three children to Kurt Vonnegut and Edith Lieber, celebrated members of the Indianapolis upper class. Kurt Sr. was a successful young architect whose father practiced the same trade, and was in fact the first architect licensed by the state of Indiana. His mother Edith grew up in the opulence of the Lieber fortune, built through the success of the P. Lieber & Company brewery in Indianapolis. Married in Indianapolis' First Unitarian Church on November 22, 1913, their wedding celebration was, "probably the biggest and most costly party which the town had ever seen or is likely to ever witness again," attended by the leading German families of the city. (*Palm Sunday* 51)

Much of what is known about Vonnegut's lineage was researched by his Uncle John Rauch, who was actually a husband of Kurt Vonnegut Sr.'s cousin, and an intimate of the Vonnegut family. His work, "An Account of the Ancestry of Kurt Vonnegut, Jr., by an Ancient Friend of His Family," was made available in the author's *Palm Sunday*. Though they were descendants of German immigrants who had arrived in America not long before the Civil War, both families enjoyed intense prosperity in the United States, due partly to diligence and partly to a good start, since Vonnegut's ancestors were well-to-do even in Germany.

"I am descended from Europeans who have been literate for a long time," Vonnegut wrote in *Palm Sunday*, his first of two autobiographical works, "who have not been slaves since the early days of the Roman games, most likely" (*Palm Sunday* 18). Like many literate Germans who emigrated to the United States in the nineteenth century, Vonnegut's forbears eschewed Christianity for Free Thinking, a humanist, atheist doctrine, and they were active enough that his great-grandfather Clemens Vonnegut, who died in 1906, published a short book on his philosophy, entitled *Instruction in Morals*. From this Vonnegut takes the epigraph for *Palm Sunday*: "Whoever entertains liberal views and chooses a consort that is captured by superstition risks his liberty and his happiness." Clemens' self-penned funeral oration, a primer in humanist thought, was printed in *Palm Sunday*. He writes:

> We cannot believe that this Being formed a human being from clay and breathed into it an Immortal Soul, and then allowed this human being to procreate millions, and then delivered them all into unspeakable misery, wretchedness and pain for all eternity. Nor can we believe that the descendants of one or two human beings will inevitably become sinners; nor do we believe that through the criminal execution of an Innocent One we may be redeemed. (194)

Even though he had not known about his great-grandfather's writings until 1976, Vonnegut adopted the precepts of Free Thinking—not only those that deny the existence of a Christian (or any other) God, but also its emphasis on human decency. So Vonnegut's fiction expounds how he believes people should behave toward one another as much as it questions the Christian ideas of

God. "How proud I became of our belief, how pigheadedly proud, even, is the most evident thing in my writing, I think" (195).

Vonnegut's parents had two children before him, Bernard and Alice, both of whom were raised in the high society the Vonneguts enjoyed, attending private schools throughout their formative years. Kurt, too, attended the private Orchard School in Indianapolis until 1936. They were raised in the arts, and developed tastes for music, painting, and literature. When the Great Depression hit the Vonnegut household, his mother envisioned making "a new fortune by writing for the slick magazines," Vonnegut said in his *Paris Review* "self-interview." "She took short story courses at night. She studied magazines the way gamblers study racing forms." Vonnegut calls her his most important influence on him as a writer (Hayman et al. 75).

The importance of the close, extended family is one of the biggest themes in Vonnegut's writing. The large, supportive family Vonnegut has espoused in his fiction and public appearances has its origins in the aegis of his boyhood Indianapolis. Though his own nuclear family grew tumultuous, he was able to envision the systems of support enjoyed by his father and his father's father before him:

> Whenever I go to Indianapolis, the same question asks itself over and over again in my head: "Where's my bed, where's my bed?" And if my father's and grandfather's ghosts still haunt that town, they must be wondering where all their buildings have gone to.... They must be wondering where all their relatives have gone to, too. They grew up in a huge extended family which is no more. I got the slightest taste of that—the big family thing. And when I went to the University of Chicago, and I heard the head of the Department of Anthropology, Robert Redfield, lecture on the folk society, which was essentially a stable, isolated extended family, he did not have to tell me how nice that could be. (Hayman et al. 101)

After thinking about it for years, Vonnegut will locate the root of many ills of society—marital problems, unattended children, the proliferation of television, to name just a few—in the absence of the big family in American culture.

Vonnegut's German ancestry, too, has shadowed his life and writing. Kurt Sr. and Edith Vonnegut were both raised in their ethnicity—fluent in German, they even studied for years in Germany. But World War I shattered many Old World ties, contributing to his father's withdrawal from the rest of the world. "My father had lost all interest in current events by the time of the first world war," Vonnegut remembered in a 1980 interview. "He lived in such a congenial world, one that treated him well as an artist, and he loved to wander about Europe and America, sketching and enjoying music. Well, when all that was smashed by the war, my father let go. He lost all interest" (Allen, *Conversations with Kurt Vonnegut* 228). In time with Kurt Sr's abandon of his European concerns, there developed an anti-German sentiment in America that made a German ancestry something to conceal during and after the Great War. His parents consciously kept Vonnegut from his German heritage. As Vonnegut put it, "They volunteered to make me ignorant and rootless as proof of their patriotism," (*Palm Sunday* 21).

Vonnegut's humor has doubtlessly contributed to his appeal, and he frequently cites its source in his family life growing up. In his fiction, jokes are foundational. He has in fact described his books as "essentially mosaics, thousands and thousands of tiny little chips all glued together, and each chip is this thing I learned to do—this thing I learned to make as a child—which is a little joke" (*Conversations* 69). He describes his joking as an altogether conscious effort on the part of himself as the baby of the family to take part in the conversations and affairs of the rest of the family:

> I got to be a joke-maker as the youngest member of my family. My sister was five years older than I was, my brother was nine years older, and at the dinner table I was the lowest ranking thing there. I could not be interesting to these vivid grownups. My sister was a sculptress and doing extremely well, my brother was a scientist, my father was an architect, and so they had really bigtime stuff to argue about. I wanted to talk to learn how to do it, to engage in

give and take, and I must have made accidental jokes at first.
Everyone does. It's a chancy thing, it's a spoonerism or something
of that sort. But anyway it stopped the adult conversation for a
minute. And I understood the terms under which I could buy my
way into conversations, small as I was. So I got awfully good at
making jokes, and I became an avid reader of humor books. I
listened to radio comedians who were brilliant during the thirties
and found out that what made them so damned funny was how
their jokes were timed. (*Conversations* 69)

To these radio comedians—and comedians in general—Vonnegut
has attributed much. Certainly as a literary influence Vonnegut
has aligned himself with the great satirists. "The function of an
artist is to respond to his own time," he told William Noble in
1972. "Voltaire, Swift and Mark Twain did it" (*Conversations* 64).
Vonnegut even named his son Mark after the great American
humorist. But it is from the radio comedians of his youth that
Vonnegut learned the registers of humor in society. From his 1973
interview with Robert Scholes:

The Depression did break people's spirits. And the comedians
who—there was one each day, at least, as Fred Allen, Jack Benny,
and so forth, you got your little dose of humor every day, and the
people did cluster around the radios to pick up an amount of
encouragement, an amount of relief. (*Conversations* 124)

By the standards of the Depression, the Vonneguts were still
wealthy, but by his teens, the market crash of 1929 and its
aftermath had severely weakened the Vonnegut's finances, and
Kurt Jr. had to attend public school. They were forced to sell the
family's china and their mansion, designed and built by Kurt Sr.
The tremendous losses of the stock market crash had been
accentuated by the closing of the Lieber brewery during
Prohibition in 1921 (and by the spendthrift lifestyle of Edith
Vonnegut's father, Albert), and the virtual non-existence of
architectural work during the Great Depression. "From the time
he was forty-five until he was sixty-one he had almost no work,"

Vonnegut recalled. (*Fates Worse Than Death* 22) During World War II, likewise, American industry devoted so much of its resources to the war machine that almost no buildings were built, making it impossible for Vonnegut's father to practice as an architect.

The economic situation the Vonneguts faced during the Great Depression proved to be mentally cataclysmic for his parents. His father had to close the architectural firm started by his own father and fire his employees. The lack of work led to a lack of purpose, and Kurt Sr. withdrew from the world and world affairs. His mother took the fall in status even more drastically. Raised with servants and employing them her whole life, Vonnegut's mother found herself at odds with the duties of running a household and raising children.

> [B]y 1930 when it was obvious that everything was gone and wasn't going to come back, I got pulled out of an elitist private school ... and sent to a public high school. Which was swell. I liked it; it was interesting. But I would go over to other kids' houses and their mothers would make cookies and say, "Want something to eat?" My mother absolutely refused to cook, and was proud of it. Somebody who would actually say, "Come on in out of the cold and have some hot soup" seemed like a very good person indeed. (*Conversations* 270)

Edith Vonnegut became depressed, sleepless, and eventually insane. "When my mother went off her rocker late at night," Vonnegut remembers in *Fates Worse Than Death,* his second "autobiographical collage," "the hatred and contempt she sprayed on my father, as gentle and innocent a man as ever lived, was without limit and pure, untainted by ideas or information" (*Fates Worse Than Death* 36). Vonnegut's later enlistment into the Army in 1943 proved too much for her. Tragically, he was approved for a special leave to go home for Mother's Day, but she committed suicide the day before he arrived.

The effects of economics and a sense of purpose on the mental well-being of individuals is a theme visited often in Vonnegut's fiction, and characters who face suicide are ubiquitous. There is surely a source for Vonnegut's overarching pessimism here, too, and his own depressive periods. David Standish asked the author about his sadness in his 1973 *Playboy* interview.

> I'm an atheist, as I said, and not into funerals—I don't like the idea of them very much—but I finally decided to go visit the graves of my parents. And so I did. There are two stones out there in Indianapolis, and I looked at those two stones side by side and I just wished—I could hear it in my head, I knew so much what I wished—that they had been happier than they were. It would have been so goddamned easy for them to be happier than they were.... I learned a bone-deep sadness from them. (*Conversations* 88–89)

Vonnegut's switch to an Indiana public school—Shortridge High School—put him in contact with the *Shortridge Daily Echo*. Shortridge was one of the first schools in the country to have a daily newspaper, and there Vonnegut reported and wrote, and by his junior year became the editor of the Tuesday edition. This was the beginning of Vonnegut's experiences in journalism, orienting him towards a career in writing, and informed the punchy, to-the-point journalistic style of his fiction.

Vonnegut has remarked that if it were not for his father's hard luck in the field of architecture, he too would have happily taken up the trade (Hayman et al. 100). He loved journalism, too, and envisioned graduating from high school and going directly to work for an Indianapolis newspaper. But Kurt Sr. did what he could to steer his son away from the arts.

> Father suggested that I become a scientist. My father himself was an architect and quite demoralized about the arts, as he hadn't made any money for ten years because of the Depression. So he told me to be a chemist, and since it was his money, I went and started to become a chemist at Cornell University. (*Conversations* 111–112)

Vonnegut's older brother Bernard had studied chemistry at MIT, and had a very successful career ahead of him, a career choice Vonnegut's father lauded for its sensibility and its distance from what he perceived the all-too-effeminate life of an architect. "[M]y father was right on the edge of the woman's world as an architect. His father had been in the same spot. So they'd collect guns and go hunting with the best of them" (*Conversations* 275). He suggests his father's extensive gun collection and frequent hunting trips was compensation for a life in the arts.

His study of the sciences surely influences much of Vonnegut's fiction, yet he scored terribly at Cornell. He describes his time there as "a boozy dream, partly because of the booze itself, and partly because I was taking courses I had no talent for" (Hayman et al. 79–80). He found diversions. He remembers fondly his fraternity life in Delta Upsilon, and he wrote columns for the student-owned newspaper. "When I got to Cornell my experiences on a daily paper—and daily high school papers were unheard of then—enabled me to become a big shot on Cornell's *Daily Sun*" (*Conversations* 196). Here he practiced his humor and wrote pacifist pieces, but enlisted in March of 1943 after the Japanese bombed Pearl Harbor. "I was flunking everything by my junior year. I was delighted to join the Army and go to war" (Hayman et al. 81).

In *Fates Worse Than Death*, Vonnegut recalls a stunt he pulled at Cornell, just before he left college for army training:

All males were required to take two years of ROTC. I was in the horse-drawn artillery, believe it or not. (That is how long ago that was.) By the end of my sophomore year the USA was at war with Germany, Italy, and Japan. I had enlisted in the Army and was waiting to be called. A Major General came to inspect us. I went to that inspection wearing every sort of medal, for swimming, for scouting, for Sunday-school attendance or whatever, that I could borrow from anyone. I may have been going nuts, since I was flunking practically everything, including ROTC.

The General asked my name but otherwise made no comment. I am sure, though, that he made a record of the incident, as he should have, and that his report shadowed me, as it should have, during my subsequent three years as a full-time soldier, ensuring that I, until the very end, would never rise above the rank of Private First Class. It served me right, and it was one of the best things that ever happened to me. (A half-educated PFC has so much to think about!)

When the war was over (forty-five years ago!), I like everybody else was entitled to wear a badge and several ribbons which were militarily correct and respectable. It is my wry satisfaction now, since I know what I did to deserve such ornaments, to regard them as no more meaningful than the borrowed trinkets that I wore at that fateful ROTC inspection so long ago. The joke at the beginning was the joke at the end. How was that for foreshadowing? (*Fates* 21)

That Vonnegut can look back derisively at his military experiences, which *Life* magazine once called "a harrowing experience in absurdity" (*Conversations* 12), is perhaps not surprising. The bulk of his comment on the war and Dresden comes from the period following the publication of *Slaughterhouse-Five,* and it may be that the therapeutic, cathartic nature of writing he has testified to in the past provided enough distance for him to make some light of the events. Moreover, though he had spent years trying to approach his capture and subsequent survival of the Allied firebombing of Dresden in writing, he has downplayed the gravity of the events themselves. "Dresden was astonishing," he told *Playboy,* "but experiences can be astonishing without changing you" (*Conversations* 94).

Leaving Cornell, Vonnegut was trained on the 240mm howitzer, "the largest mobile field piece in use at that time." An outdated monstrosity as artillery goes, Vonnegut jokes that its three hundred-pound shell "would come floating out like the Goodyear blimp. If we had a stepladder, we could have painted 'Fuck Hitler' on the shell as it left the gun." He called it "[t]he ultimate terror weapon... of the Franco-Prussian War" (Hayman et al. 60–61).

Even though he took his training on this weapon, the Army sent him back to school. At the Carnegie Institute of Technology and the University of Tennessee he took courses in mechanical engineering. He was then sent to Europe as a battalion scout for the 106th Infantry Division, despite having received no training for the infantry:

> Battalion scouts were elite troops, see. There were only six in each battalion, and nobody was very sure about what they were supposed to do. So we would march over to the rec room every morning, and play ping-pong and fill out applications for Officer Candidate School. (Hayman et al., 61)

The 106th reached the European theatre in November of 1944, just in time for the huge December German offensive—its last on the Western front—known as the Battle of the Bulge. The Americans took tremendous losses. "My last mission as a scout was to find our own artillery.... Things got so bad that we were finally looking for our own stuff" (Hayman et al. 62). A *Life* magazine article published in the wake of *Slaughterhouse-Five* shows the beginning of his problems:

> For what he believes to have been 11 days, he wandered around as an infantry scout, improvising his own tactics (all his training had been in the artillery), not knowing where the lines were or whether there were any lines, and living with death in a catatonic embrace. (*Conversations* 12)

Captured, he was taken to a prison camp for a time, then sent to Dresden, where thousands of other POW's were being held. Contrary to some published accounts, Dresden was not an open city—a city known to house no troops and support no war industries, and hence not classified as an enemy target. It was, however, home to many refugees and few standing troops, and so was generally regarded to be "safe" from attack. Because of his rank as a Private, the Geneva Convention dictated that he had to work for his keep as a prisoner. "There were about a hundred of us in our particular work group, and we were put out as contract labor to a factory that was making vitamin-enriched malt syrup for pregnant women" (*Mother Night* vi).

Dresden was "the first fancy city I'd ever seen" (Hayman et al. 66), "a highly ornamented city, like Paris" (*Conversations* 163). "The damned sirens would go off and we'd hear some other city getting it—*whump a whump a whumpa whump*. We never expected to get it" (Hayman et al., 66). "There were no air-raid shelters, just ordinary cellars, because a raid was not expected and the war was almost over," he told interviewers Joe Bellamy and John Casey in 1974. He also told them how a firestorm is created:

> Waves and waves of planes come over carrying high explosives which open roofs, make lots of kindling, and drive the firemen underground. Then they take hundreds of thousands of little incendiary bombs (the size had been reduced from a foot and a half to the size of a shotgun shell by the end of the war) and scatter them. Then more high explosives until all the little fires join up into one apocalyptic flame with tornadoes around the edges sucking more and more, feeding the inferno. (*Conversations* 163)

This happened the night of February 13–14, 1945. The *New York Times* reported details of the event on February 15th:

> Dresden was hit three times within fifteen hours—twice by the RAF in a 1,400-plane operation Tuesday night that started the assault rolling, and again by Britain-based bombers of the Eighth Air Force, which staged a 2,250-plane daylight follow-up....
>
> Eight hundred RAF bombers struck Dresden in two attacks, the first at 10 P.M. Tuesday, London time, the second three hours later. They dropped nearly 650,000 incendiary bombs, hundreds of two-ton block busters and a number of four-ton ones.
>
> Smoke surged up three miles in the sky and flames were seen by returning fliers 200 miles away—which indicated they must have been a beacon to the Russian troops just east of Dresden.

The Germans reported the city as "a heap of ruins" by February the 16th, and reported 20,000 deaths. That figure was raised to 70,000 by the 17th. A German radio announcer declared on the night of March 4, 1945, that the city of Dresden no longer existed. For some time the casualty count remained ambiguous because of the large number of refugees in the city, but history generally accepted the figure offered by David Irving in *The Destruction of Dresden* at 135,000 people, and which Vonnegut used as a source for *Slaughterhouse-Five*. (Irving later revised his own figure to no more than 35,000 in a letter to the *Times of London* in 1966; the number is still uncertain.)

Vonnegut, a few dozen other prisoners, and a handful of guards became part of a very small number of Dresden survivors, finding shelter in a meat locker three stories below the streets of Dresden—Slaughterhouse-Five. When they surfaced Vonnegut was given the job of digging for corpses in the rubble, "as a sanitary measure." But the number of the dead was so great, and the city so ruined, that he describes it as a "terribly elaborate Easter egg hunt." Things would get worse:

> After a few days the city began to smell, and a new technique was invented. Necessity is the mother of invention. We would bust into the shelter, gather up valuables from people's laps without attempting to identify them, and turn the valuables over to guards. Then soldiers would come in with a flame thrower and stand in the door and cremate the people inside. Get the gold and jewelry out and then burn everybody inside. (Hayman et al. 67)

After the general surrender in May 1945, his German guards vanished. "Vonnegut again wandered between lines for several days, until he was repatriated by the Russians on May 22" (Klinkowitz, *Vonnegut in America* 13). He spent some time in a military hospital in Europe. "I was phenomenally hungry for about six months. There wasn't nearly enough to eat..." (*Conversations* 94-95). After having gained back some of the 41 pounds he lost while a prisoner of war, Vonnegut returned to Indianapolis. He was awarded the Purple Heart for frostbite. Vonnegut remembers in *Timequake* that, Like Hemingway, he "never shot a human being" during the war:

When I got back from my war, my uncle Dan clapped me on the back, and he bellowed, "You're a man now!"

I damn near killed my first German. (*Timequake* 70)

He married Jane Cox, his high school sweetheart on September 1, 1945, and moved to Chicago to pursue a Master's degree in anthropology in December of that year. Vonnegut relished his studies there. He recalled in a speech he gave to the National Institute of Arts and Letters (published in his first work of non-fiction, *Wampeters, Foma, & Granfalloons*) that his son once asked him what the happiest moment of his life had been:

The happiest day of my life, so far, was in October of 1945. I had just been discharged from the United States Army, which was still an honorable organization in those Walt Disney times. I had just been admitted to the Department of Anthropology at the University of Chicago.

At last! I was going to study man! (*Wampeters, Foma, & Granfalloons* 177)

Vonnegut's study of social anthropology put him in contact with Dr. Robert Redfield, who "became the most satisfying teacher in my life" (*Wampeters* 178). Redfield's idea of the folk society—behaviors characteristic of all primitive societies, including small, intimate groups of people, communicating exclusively with one another, sharing an oral history, treating each other equally as people—was wholly adopted into Vonnegut's world view. It would be the scientific skeleton he used to advance his own idea that a large, supportive family would ease many modern societal anxieties. His fantastic solution is the center of Wilbur Daffodil-11 Swain's presidential campaign in *Slapstick*: issue citizens a new middle name that would randomly include them in a family thousands strong.

Left-leaning faculty at Chicago were also advancing cultural relativism when Vonnegut arrived in the forties, and here again he felt right at home. "Religions were exhibited and studied like the Rube Goldberg inventions I'd always thought they were," he said for the *Paris Review*. "We weren't allowed to find one culture superior to another" (*Conversations* 81). Such claims of the universal efficacy of cultures and religions "confirmed [his] atheism," and became the centerpiece for one of his best and best-known novels, *Cat's Cradle*. "A first-grader should understand that his culture isn't a rational invention," he told *Playboy*, "that there are thousands of other cultures and they all work pretty well; that all cultures function on faith rather than on truth; that there are lots of alternatives to our own society" (*Conversations* 104). *Cat's Cradle* built a new religion, Bokononism, on "harmless untruths" that affect happiness on practitioners. It demonstrated (among other things) that truth need not be prerequisite to a functioning religion. The novel brought the precepts of cultural relativism from the pages of scholarly journals to a freethinking collegiate youth:

> Of course, now cultural relativity is fashionable—and that probably has something, to do with my popularity among young people. But it's more than fashionable—it's defensible, attractive. It's also a source of hope. It means we don't have to continue this way if we don't like it. (*Conversations* 104)

For all he learned and loved in the Anthropology Department at Chicago, Vonnegut did not earn his degree. His Master's thesis, which he described as "my prettiest contribution to my culture" (*Palm Sunday* 312), was entitled *Fluctuations Between Good and Evil in Simple Tales*. The text has apparently been lost, but Vonnegut would give the basics in a chalkboard session at the end of his public speaking engagements over the years, and has reprinted the most important points in *Palm Sunday*.

His method was to gather stories from wide-ranging cultures— Native American Indian stories, Biblical narratives, even short stories from the slick magazines he would come to write for—and plot them on a graph. Good or bad fortune was plotted on the x-axis, while time figured on the y-axis, from beginning to end. A story's "shape" could thus be compared with those of other cultures. His most compelling discovery was that Cinderella, which he notes is one of our culture's most enduring stories—"at this very moment, a thousand writers must be telling that story again in one form or another," (*Palm Sunday* 315)—bears precisely the same shape as the creation, fall, and redemption told by the Old and New Testaments. "I was thrilled to discover that years ago, and I am just as thrilled today," he writes (*Palm Sunday* 316). *Fluctuations* was unanimously rejected by the University of Chicago. Ironically, a new dean at the University of Chicago accepted *Cat's Cradle* as a Master's thesis and granted him a degree in 1972, after he had achieved national recognition.

Vonnegut had by now attended four different institutions of higher learning and by 1947 had nothing but a high school diploma to find gainful employ. He had done some work in journalism in Chicago, working as a beat reporter for the Chicago City News Bureau, an agency that sold police and accident reports to the newspapers of the area. He set down one event—the first he had to cover—in *Slaughterhouse-Five*, two decades later. In the novel, the story serves to prime the reader to expect any kind of source in the book; at the same time it demonstrates the human capacity for apathy he has witnessed firsthand:

> [T]he first story I covered… was about a young veteran who had taken a job running an old fashioned elevator in an office building. The elevator door on the first floor was ornamental iron lace. Iron ivy snaked in and out of the holes. There was an iron twig with two iron lovebirds perched upon it.
>
> This veteran decided to take his car into the basement, and he closed the door and started down, but his wedding ring was caught in all the ornaments. So he was hoisted into the air and the floor of the car went down, dropped out from under him, and the top of the car squished him. So it goes.
>
> So I phoned this in, and the woman who was going to cut the stencil asked me, "What did his wife say?"
>
> "She doesn't know yet," I said. "It just happened."
>
> "Call her up and get a statement."
>
> "What?"
>
> "Tell her you're Captain Finn of the Police Department. Say

you have some sad news. Give her the news, and see what she says."

So I did. She said-about what you would expect her to say. There was a baby. And so on. (*Slaughterhouse-Five* 9)

Contrary to Vonnegut's own situation, Vonnegut's older brother Bernard was enjoying success and a promising career as a research scientist. In 1947 he held a research position with General Electric in their Schenectady facility, and through him Vonnegut found a job working in their public relations department. He moved his small but growing family—son Mark was born that year and daughter Edith arrived in 1949—to Schenectady and took the post for $90 a week.

He was twenty-five, and had never written so much as a short story. But here his ambition, his need to support his family, his ethical reservations about his work at General Electric, and his creativity, came together to advance Vonnegut into a career as a freelance writer.

CHAPTER TWO

From General Electric to Germany

Dear Pop:

I sold my first story to Collier's. *Received my check ($750 minus a 10% agent's commission) yesterday noon. It now appears that two more of my works have a good chance of being sold in the near future.*

I think I'm on my way. I've deposited my first check in a savings account and, as and if I sell more, will continue to do so until I have the equivalent of one year's pay at GE. Four more stories will do it nicely, with cash to spare (something we never had before). I will then quit this goddamn nightmare job, and never take another one so long as I live, so help me God.

I'm happier than I've been in a good many years.

Love.

K.

—Letter to Kurt Vonnegut Sr.
October 28, 1949, *Fates Worse Than Death*

IN 1979, TEN YEARS AFTER the publication of *Slaughterhouse-Five*, Vonnegut spoke to a crowd at an anti-nuke rally in Washington, D.C.:

The people who play with such chemicals are so dumb!

They are also vicious. How vicious it is of them to tell us as little as possible about the hideousness of nuclear weapons and power plants!

And, among all the dumb and vicious people, who jeopardizes all life on earth with hearts so light? I suggest to you that it is those who will lie for the nuclear industries, or who will teach their executives how to lie convincingly—for a fee. I speak of certain lawyers and communicators, and all public relations experts. The so-called profession of public relations, an American invention, stands entirely disgraced today. (*Palm Sunday* 71)

Kurt Vonnegut found himself in public relations in 1947. "Because of all this background in science that I had had, they made me a flak, a publicity man for the research laboratory there, which is an excellent industrial research laboratory" (*Conversations* 112). General Electric's research lab was one where new ideas and products were ubiquitous, and what he saw there impressed the 23-year-old. He had grown up in awe of the sciences; years later he would write in a piece for the Swedish newspaper *Aftonbladet,* "an enthusiasm for technological cures for almost all forms of human discontent was the only religion of my family during the Great Depression, when I first got to know that family well" (*Palm Sunday* 69). Vonnegut talked about these early days in a 1993 interview at the home of Ollie Lyon, a lifelong friend and fellow public relations writer for GE in the late forties: "I was a child of the Great Depression.... And to us a job has always been a job. If you got a job, there would be a party and everything. Then about midnight, somebody would ask what the job was" (Reed and Leeds, 37).

If for a time he was happy for the work, he came to dislike it, eventually describing the profession in the terms above. He was particularly at odds with the compromises in truth he sometimes had to engender; themes of artists who sacrifice their talents for the sake of propaganda lace Vonnegut's novels, most ostensibly in *Mother Night* (1961). But it was the effects of technology that made Vonnegut most uncomfortable as a corporate front man.

The incredible destruction of World War II set off his disillusion with what was passing for "progress" in post-War America. "I learned how vile that religion of mine could be when the atomic bomb was dropped on Hiroshima" (*Palm Sunday* 69). General Electric's research labs were at the forefront of new ideas and technology, and he saw first-hand how technology came to the detriment of parts of society:

> One day I came across an engineer who had developed a milling machine that could be run by punch cards. Now at the time, milling machinists were among the best paid machinists in the world, and yet this damned machine could do as good a job as any of the machinists ever could. I looked around, then, and found looms and spinning machines and a number of textile devices all being run the same way and, well, the implications were sensational. (*Conversations* 199)

These negative experiences at General Electric have their place as one of the driving factors behind his decision to turn to writing. Others Vonnegut worked with in public relations were also aspiring writers, but few put in as much time. "I disliked my job at General Electric and in order to quit and hang on to my family I wrote short stories on weekends and nights" (*Conversations* 51).

But besides his general discontent with his job, Vonnegut cites other reasons for his turn to writing. He felt he had something to say after witnessing the destruction of Dresden in the war, though for a time, he wasn't sure if he had seen anything special:

> When I got home (I was a writer since I had been on the Cornell Sun except that was the extent of my writing) I thought of writing my war story, too. All my friends were home; they'd had wonderful adventures, too. I went down to the newspaper office, the Indianapolis News, and I looked to find out what they had about Dresden. There was an item about half an inch long, which said our planes had been over Dresden and two had been lost. And so I figured, well, this really was the most minor sort of detail in World

War II.... But every so often I would meet a European and we would be talking about the war and I would say I was in Dresden; he'd be astonished that I'd been there, and he'd always want to know more. Then a book by David Irving was published about Dresden, saying it was the largest massacre in European history. I said, by God, I saw something after all! I would try to write my story, whether it was interesting or not, and try to make something out of it. (Hayman et al. 69)

The story, of course, would become *Slaughterhouse-Five*, though it wouldn't appear until 1969, twenty years later.

Vonnegut also cites his mother's failed writing career as a reason he took up the craft. "She was a good writer," Vonnegut admits for the *Paris Review*, "but she had no talent for the vulgarity the slick magazines required. Fortunately, I was loaded with vulgarity, so when I grew up, I was able to make her dream come true" (Hayman et al. 76).

In February of 1950, Vonnegut's first short fiction was published in *Collier's* magazine. His early success was partly due to healthy demand for creative fiction at the time (venues like *Collier's* and the *Saturday Evening Post* would publish five or more short stories a week), and partly due to the willingness of editors to nurture young authors. "When I was working for General Electric, I wrote a story, 'Report on the Barnhouse Effect,' the first story I ever wrote. I mailed it off to *Collier's*. Knox Burger was fiction editor there. Knox told me what was wrong and how to fix it. I did what he said, and he bought the story for seven-hundred fifty dollars, six weeks pay at GE" (Hayman et al. 96).

Knox Burger would do much to aid Vonnegut in his early career, including introducing the young writer to Kenneth Littauer, an agent and former *Collier's* editor, and Max Wilkinson, a story editor for MGM. Vonnegut contends that Burger "discovered and encouraged more good young writers than any other editor of his time" (Hayman et al. 96), and it is to Burger that Vonnegut dedicates his collection of short stories, *Welcome to the Monkey House*.

Ten days older than I am.
He has been a very good
Father to me.

But it was Littauer who worked most closely with the young author on technique and craft. "I was a very earnest student writer and had a teacher," Vonnegut later said in an interview, "Kenneth Littauer, an old-time magazine and editor.... I learned from Littauer about pace and point of view, things that are discussed in *Writer's Digest*, decent and honorable things to know" (*Conversations* 158).

Many critics maintain that "Report on the Barnhouse Effect" is one of Vonnegut's best fictions. Written in a journalistic style comfortable to Vonnegut, it tells the story of Professor Arthur Barnhouse, who discovers what he calls *dynamopsychism* (the "Barnhouse Effect"), which is the ability to move objects with his mind. "By my calculations," the narrator explains, "the professor was about fifty-five times more powerful than a Nagasaki-type atomic bomb at the time he went into hiding" (*Welcome to the Monkey House* 174). Barnhouse is quickly seen as an asset to hawks in the armed services, so he goes underground, using his power to effect peace by destroying weapons in countries around the world. Barnhouse's death means the imminent return of weapons and war, yet when the story ends we know his assistant, through whom the story is told, has attained some of the powers held by the erstwhile professor.

Even in this his first of stories, Vonnegut explores the nature of scientific progress and its relationship to destruction and war. That the world's arsenal will be inevitably rebuilt unless checked—that the government rejects the use of Barnhouse's powers to bring rain to arid lands and prefers instead its use in military tactics—shows his essential pessimism about the human condition. Many of Vonnegut's characteristic narrative techniques, too, first show up in "Barnhouse." A first person narrator who maintains some distance throughout the story, but who jumps into the action by the end will become one of Vonnegut's most successful ways of telling.

"Report on the Barnhouse Effect" contains biographical

elements worth noting. In *The Short Fiction of Kurt Vonnegut*, Vonnegut scholar Peter Reed points out that:

> Barnhouse's suggestion for moving clouds to drought-stricken areas echoes Vonnegut's brother Bernard's pioneer work in cloud seed. The narrator is a veteran of overseas service and works in a laboratory. And the prediction of Barnhouse's mortality because he comes of short-lived stock sounds reminiscent of Vonnegut's own tendency to make life predictions for himself and others based on parental lifespans. (Reed 30)

Vonnegut injects himself quite often into his works, a technique that pays the greatest dividends in *Slaughterhouse-Five* but which continues to his last novel, *Timequake*.

"If 'Report on the Barnhouse Effect' borders on science fiction, or science fiction with parapsychological overtones," Reed suggests, "the next story, 'Thanosphere,' goes further" (30). And so would many Vonnegut stories. He in fact seems drawn to the genre—almost against his will—and in interviews and essays he appears taken aback when he is classified as such. "There was no avoiding it," Vonnegut resolves in his 1973 *Playboy* interview, "since the General Electric company *was* science fiction" (*Conversations* 193).

PLAYER PIANO

Vonnegut wrote in a 1965 article for the *New York Times*: "Years ago I was working in Schenectady for General Electric, completely surrounded by machines, so I wrote a novel about people and machines, and machines frequently got the best of it, as machines will…. And I learned from reviewers that I was a science fiction writer" (September 5, 1965).

Having published several stories, Vonnegut left his steady GE paycheck in 1951, moving his family to Cape Cod. *Player Piano* appeared in 1952, and was marketed exclusively to science fiction consumers. That his first novel was printed directly to paperback (like countless other science fiction novels of the time) loomed large over his work for the duration of his career. He struggled first to gain a wider recognition for his work, to break out of the loyal but limited science fiction following; but even once his writing gained popular attention, Vonnegut would meet yet more resistance from academics, some of whom considered him little more than a slick writer who got lucky.

Like many of the short stories Vonnegut was writing at the time, *Player Piano* finds its genesis in the remarkable speed with which American industry raced forward after World War II. Its protagonist, Paul Proteus, is a 35-year-old executive who ought to relish his position in the "ruling class" of the technocracy Vonnegut describes, yet in spite of the utopian talk of nearly everyone around him, Proteus has reservations about how good things really are:

> Objectively, Paul tried to tell himself, things really were better than ever. For once, after the great bloodbath of the war, the world really was cleared of unnatural terrors—mass starvation, mass imprisonment, mass torture, mass murder. Objectively, know-how and world law were getting their long-awaited chance to turn earth into an altogether pleasant and convenient place in which to sweat out Judgment Day. (*Player Piano* 14)

Vonnegut explained the creative impetus for this project in a 1993 interview: "What if all economically useful work could be done more cheaply and satisfactorily by machines than by human beings?" (Reed and Leeds, 36). In *Player Piano*, Vonnegut postulates that the mechanization of society exists to the detriment of human dignity.

War is central to the plot of *Player Piano*. This is evident from the first lines, which allude to Julius Caesar's first commentary on the Gallic Wars:

> Ilium, New York, is divided into three parts.
>
> In the northwest are the managers and engineers and civil servants and a few professional people; in the northeast are the machines; and in the south, across the Iroquois River, is the area known locally as Homestead, where almost all of the people live. (9)

The story takes place ten years after the Third World War, and it figures heavily in the novel as the reason society mechanized so quickly. This begins a long line of Vonnegutian novels where war—or apocalyptic destruction of some form—is presented intrinsic to technological or scientific advance. Vonnegut scholar David Seed notes that Ilium is connected to a history of war, and that war is presented numerous times in the novel as an agent of social change. This social change, this future exists only at the expense of democracy. Vonnegut tells us that it was know-how that won the war, that an industrial machine functioning without manpower saved democracy. But ironically this post-war society is anything but democratic. The men and women that went away to fight returned to find that their jobs were now being done exclusively by machines, and so resigned themselves to an idle and inconsequential life in Homestead. Almost everyone has two choices for employment: join the Army, or work in the Reclamation and Reconstruction Corps doing menial labor. The fictional Ilium, New York, demonstrates the segregation of this America even in its geography, with a river separating the elite from the latter-day proletariat. The novel questions the human cost of this environment, absent societal ills (as Proteus tries to remind himself) notwithstanding.

By the same mechanics of progress that put the populace out of work, the few employed managers and engineers find their positions threatened as well. A second industrial revolution saw the replacement of white collar minds by computers. This accounts for most of the people living across the river in Homestead. Paul Proteus realizes that an imminent "Third Revolution in Industry," in which artificial intelligence would replace brass in even the highest echelons of the corporate world, presents the greatest danger to this "utopia."

Paul's suspicions of the virtues of an automated society arrive as he's being considered for a hefty promotion—the preoccupation of his mechanical wife, Anita—and coincide with the return of an old friend, Ed Finnerty, who had moved on to bigger and better things in Washington. Fed up with the system, Finnerty has quit his post, and serves to show Paul the possibility of rebellion.

Opposite Finnerty is Paul's boss Kroner, an old friend of Paul's late father, who was "the nation's first National Industrial, Commercial, Communications, Foodstuffs, and Resources Director, a position approached in importance only by the presidency of the United States" (*Player Piano* 10).

Finnerty will take an uncertain Proteus "underground"—a recurring move in Vonnegut's literature—and introduces him to a rebels called the Ghost Shirt Society, a Luddite group of sorts dedicated to smashing machines. Kroner, meanwhile, is presented as a surrogate father, drawing Paul toward complicity with the corporate technocracy.

The novel is punctuated by observations from the visiting potentate, the Shah of Bratpuhr, "spiritual leader of the 6,000,000 members of the Kolhouri sect," who "had left his military and spiritual fastness in the mountains to see what he could learn in the most powerful nation on earth for the good of his people" (26). The Shah is the first of many characters in Vonnegut's novels that exist to add an outsider's commentary to the situations presented in the story. Partly for his childlike—if often accurate—observations on what he sees in America, the Shah is a major source of the comical material in *Player Piano*. The use of humor and hyperbole has been a part of Vonnegut's writing since his high school and college days, and it becomes a hallmark in his novels.

Other characters in Vonnegut's novels become mouthpieces for the author, and in *Player Piano*, it is the chaplain of the Reclamation and Reconstruction Corps, James Lasher, who provides anthropological explanations for the society we see, and adds perspective by lending insight into, say, the relationship of the nineteenth century Plains Indians to the masses in Homestead. No doubt informed by Vonnegut's graduate work at the University of Chicago, characters like Lasher theorize on the circumstances and then tell us about them. It is a role assumed in Vonnegut's later novels by his surrogate, Kilgore Trout.

With one foot in the Ghost Shirt Society and the other in corporate brass, Proteus is asked to be a spy by the current National Industrial, Commercial, Communications, Foodstuffs, and Resources Director, Dr. Frances Gelhorne, through his contacts with Finnerty. He is to be "fired," infiltrate the group, and gather information for Gelhorne. Disgusted, Proteus quits, though his resignation is taken as enthusiasm for the role. Paul is drugged by Finnerty and Lasher, though his heart is with them anyway, and at their behest he becomes a Messiah to the Ghost Shirt Society. Thus Paul becomes a double agent, a scheme Vonnegut would often revisit in his novels, allowing a character to see things that are often overlooked by others. This features most heavily in *Mother Night*, where almost every character is operating under more than one identity. Paul is captured by Kroner's men and put on trial for treason. At the end of the novel the Ghost Shirts do lead a rebellion, though the drunken mob is quickly quelled. "Like most satires," writes William Rodney Allen in *Understanding Kurt Vonnegut*, "the novel concludes with the world in pretty much the same old mess" (35).

Player Piano is generally read as a satire of the post-war optimism of the 50's, when the industrial inertia that carried the United States through the war continued into peacetime. At the time of publication, however, it was received as little more than mediocre science fiction, and Vonnegut's harshest critics still see the book as just that. Clearly, though, Vonnegut is making a statement about the blind speed of post-war industrialization, along with the perceived willingness of American culture to embrace this movement.

Vonnegut also parodies other aspects of the world he found himself writing in. He plays into the fifties fascination with Freud and psychoanalysis in describing the corporate state in often sexual terms. Kroner is presented as a father figure to everyone in the Eastern Division, though Paul is most sensitive to this role, perhaps since Kroner was friends with his own father. At his trial, Paul admits to being the leader of the Ghost Shirt Society, but the prosecutor argues that Paul is suffering from an Oedipus complex, and so his rebellion against the corporate state was actually one against his father (an argument Proteus accepts). The McCarthyesque trial indicates Vonnegut's larger satire of anticommunist hysteria. William Rodney Allen notes several lexical turns that allude to this:

Lasher refers to those in the movement as 'fellow travelers,' a phrase for communists widely recognized in the 1950's. Paul feels the effects of being "blacklisted" in the way many suspected communists did in McCarthy's time, when they suddenly could not find work. When Paul returns to Ilium and begins to frequent the Homestead Bar, where he met Lasher, he is drugged by Finnerty and Lasher with "truth serum," an obsessive concern of anticommunists in the 1950s who feared brainwashing techniques involving drugging the victim, then submitting him to communist indoctrination. (*Understanding Kurt Vonnegut* 32)

Considering, then, that so much of *Player Piano* takes its cues from the 50's America Vonnegut saw, it is not as much a science fiction novel as it is an exaggeration of the times. Vonnegut is not attempting to show us the future, like Huxley and Orwell in *Brave New World* and *1984*, but to make a statement about the present by hyperbole. With his first novel, Vonnegut speaks of the dangers of technological advance and war, of the relationship between meaningful work and dignity, and—since the rebellion does indeed fail at the end—his skepticism of mass movements, even if he is on their side.

His next novel, *The Sirens of Titan,* would not appear until 1959, seven years later. Vonnegut published twenty-seven stories in the years between these novels, though despite appearing regularly in *Collier's* and the *Saturday Evening Post,* by 1954 he was taking various jobs to supplement his income. He taught English at the Hopefield School in Sandwich, Massachusetts. He did freelance public relations writing, specifically for the K. Thomas Chirurgy ad agency which, as an industrial account, utilized his experience at General Electric. He opened one of the first Saab dealerships in the United States. He also worked on a second novel titled "Upstairs and Downstairs," though that work would never be finished.

Collier's capsized later in the decade, publishing its last issue on January 4, 1957. Vonnegut has always expressed concern about the imbalance between supply and demand for printed fiction, citing "that goddamn machine, television, which is the principle teacher here" (Reed and Leeds, 29) as the prime culprit. Finding less outlets for his writing, Vonnegut turned toward more exclusively science fiction venues such as *Galaxy* and *Fantasy* as a source for income. Along with the 1954 retitle of *Player Piano* as *Utopia-14*, it is the "hack" writing Vonnegut produced in this period that would tinge his name among later critics. In his 1977 treatment of Vonnegut's novels, Richard Giannone writes that:

> When he was serious, that work was met with misunderstanding. As a rule, misjudgment is not surprising for innovative writers; and as for Vonnegut, who had an active commercial reputation to color the reaction to his work, a misreading of his deeper intention is expected.... We would do well, however, not to interpret Vonnegut's publishing history in light of his present wealthy eminence with its special prerogatives, and to resist the urge to turn his publishers into villains and his motives into artistic compromises. Vonnegut needed the money, which he earned by writing. (Giannone 6-7)

Harsher critics aside, Vonnegut himself seems to focus on this part of his career, as themes of artists who do compromise their talents—for a variety of reasons—pepper many of his novels.

The death of Vonnegut's father in October 1957 was the first personal tragedy to rail the author in the late fifties. A year later, his sister Alice died of lung cancer at the age of 41; her death came just one day after her husband, John Adams, was killed in a train crash. The Vonneguts adopted three of their four children (the youngest, at one year of age, was raised by a cousin of the father), adding to three of their own. With six children and a desiccating market for his short stories, Vonnegut would turn again to the novel.

THE SIRENS OF TITAN

The fantastic tale of *The Sirens of Titan* (1959) was made up on the spot at a cocktail party, as Richard Todd wrote in the *New York Times Magazine*.

It began, Vonnegut said, at a party, when a publishing house editor asked, "Why don't you write another book?" Vonnegut said, "Well, I have an idea for one." "Tell me about it," said the editor, and they went into a bedroom. "I had no idea at all for a book," Vonnegut recalls, "but I started talking and told him the story of *Sirens of Titan* [sic]. Every mother's favorite child is the one that's delivered by natural childbirth. *Sirens of Titan* is that kind of book" (*Conversations* 35)

The Sirens of Titan is a helter-skelter space odyssey that races its dual protagonists all over the solar system. Like *Player Piano*, it was written directly to paperback contract, and with its provocative cover, sold on drugstore checkout shelves as a "dirty" book. Even though today *The Sirens of Titan* is an integral title in the Vonnegut canon, it is, after all, an early novel, and it reads as such. "Not surprisingly," Allen writes, "the *Sirens of Titan* [sic] showed the ill effects of Vonnegut's long layoff from novel writing since *Player Piano*. While *Player Piano* is a tightly focused satire of corporate life, *The Sirens of Titan* finally lacks a coherent center" (*Understanding Kurt Vonnegut* 35).

Certainly *Player Piano* and *The Sirens of Titan* are worlds apart. *Sirens* begins with the richest man in the world, Malachi Constant, fed up with his life of booze and women, being told an extraordinary prophecy by one Winston Niles Rumfoord. Rumfoord, we find out, has by galactic accident entered a "chrono-synclastic infundibulum," a Vonnegutian whimsy. In the preface for his 1970 play *Happy Birthday, Wanda June*, he describes it as the "mathematical point where all opinions, no matter how contradictory, harmonized" (*Happy Birthday, Wanda June* ix). Due to flying his spaceship into one of these things, Rumfoord (and his dog) "are scattered far and wide, not just through space, but through time, too" (*The Sirens of Titan* 14-15), which lets him see all events of time—including the future.

Rumfoord tells Constant that he will go to Mars with Beatrice, Rumfoord's wife, and that Constant will father a child by her. Despite efforts by Malachi and Beatrice to avoid this fate, all efforts are futile, because "everything that has ever been will always be, and everything that ever will be has always been" (*Sirens* 26). (This Tralfamadorian view of time, and the fatalism inherent in it, prefigures Vonnegut's use of the construct in *Slaughterhouse-Five*.) Often described as a space opera, the action in *Sirens* includes just about every cliché the sci-fi genre has to offer. Kidnapped and brainwashed by Martians, Constant becomes a pawn in the planned invasion of earth; a trip to Mercury introduces strange creatures called harmoniums, and we meet giant bluebirds on Titan.

We find out that Rumfoord has orchestrated the whole convoluted series of events, using his power to establish a new religion, the Church of God the Utterly Indifferent. Tony Tanner notes in his foundational criticism of Vonnegut's novels that Rumfoord, "with his new-found power to arrange things to suit his patterns, to handle time and space as he pleases and put people where he wants them...is a suitably fantastic analogue of Vonnegut himself, who is doing just that in his book" (Tanner 298). His Messiah is Malachi, who carries to earth his message of human insignificance in the universe, that free will is a preposterous notion, that everything is determined by chance. "I was a victim of a series of accidents, as are we all" (*Sirens* 229), Malachi tells the world.

Even the manipulative Rumfoord is the pawn of greater forces. (Rumfoord, incidentally, is the first embodiment of Vonnegut's use of the "historical" character. He resembles Franklin Delano Roosevelt not only in appearance, but by exaggeration and behavior. Just as Roosevelt enacted his huge and controlling New Deal in the interest of raising the standard of living, Rumfoord uses his powers to manipulate people for what he feels is their own good.) Ironically, Rumfoord—along with most of human history—is all part of the plan of a robot race called the Tralfamadorians to carry a message from one side of the universe to the other, whose messenger, Salo, broke down on Saturn's moon Titan. Achievements of humanity are explained as attempts by the Tralfamadorians to contact Salo. Stonehenge and the Great Wall of China tell Salo to 'be patient,' or that replacement parts are on the way. The trivialization of human existence is underscored by the Tralfamadorian message itself: "Greetings."

Clearly Vonnegut is satirizing religious fundamentalism in *The Sirens of Titan*. Instead of placing events as meaningful extensions of God's will, the Church of God the Utterly Indifferent preaches the place of meaningless luck in all events. But even though belief systems are futile in terms of efficacy, like the Ghost Shirt Society of *Player Piano*, they're shown as crucial to establishing a sense of purpose in individuals. "Religious creeds are mendacious but nevertheless necessary inventions that cannot explain the meaning of a world which has no meaning," Peter Freese has it, "but that are necessary to provide man with the sense of purpose and direction without which he cannot live" (Reed and Leeds 150). The Church of God the Utterly Indifferent is thus a precursor to Vonnegut's larger examination of the function of religion in *Cat's Cradle*.

Freese estimates another message in *Sirens*: that "scientific attempts at understanding and mastering the universe inadvertently lead to disaster and self-extermination." Cataclysm and destruction are everywhere in Vonnegut's fiction, and these disasters are intrinsically tied to the proliferation of science and technology. And since human beings cannot help but attempt to understand their world, an essentially pessimistic outlook is advanced in almost all of Vonnegut's novels.

If it is surprising to find such deep questions on the nature of human existence in a book whose original cover depicted "machine monsters and semi-nude young women tumbling together in an asteroid belt" (Klinkowitz, *Kurt Vonnegut* 40), it is even more surprising to find attempts to answer those questions. Perhaps the best formulation of Vonnegut's post-Christian ethics, his attempt to rationalize existence in lieu of religion, is Malachi Constant's resolution that "the purpose of human life, no matter who is controlling it, is to love whoever is around to be loved" (*Sirens* 313). One of the few bright spots on the dim palette of Vonnegut's fiction is the place of decency, humanity, and kindness in a *modus vivendi*.

William Allen calls *The Sirens of Titan* a worthwhile failure, since it at least introduces the reader to elements of Vonnegut's writing style that would become his shibboleths (*Understanding*

Kurt Vonnegut 41). Short, simple paragraphs, an abundance of jokes, and a fabric of metafictional tropes (including his insistence that "all persons, places, and events in this book are real") would become Vonnegut mainstays.

MOTHER NIGHT

It is easy to view *Mother Night* (1962) as a complete departure from Vonnegut's previous writing—with its rather mundane plot (relatively speaking, of course) surrounding a man who works as both a German propagandist and an American spy during World War II—but this view leaves out a number of more domestic short stories he wrote in the dozen years before its publication.

Mother Night, too, was written under paperback contract, and many readers mistook it for a nonfiction confessional novel about the war, the likes of which were in vogue at the time. Allen attributes the striking contrast between "the unfocused, even sprawling quality of *The Sirens of Titan* and the tautness of *Mother Night*" to the structure and direction provided by the first-person point of view (*Understanding Kurt Vonnegut* 44–45), a form which brought Vonnegut success as early as his first story, "Report on the Barnhouse Effect."

The protagonist, Howard W. Campbell, Jr., is an American born in Schenectady, New York, whose father was an engineer for General Electric. His father's job took the family to Germany in 1923, when he was eleven years old; he assimilated to German society, eventually taking a German wife and writing plays in the German language. When the Second World War broke out his parents left the country, but Campbell stayed on, and through the war he worked "as a writer and broadcaster of Nazi propaganda to the English-speaking world" (*Mother Night* 32–33). Yet he also acted as an American agent, sending coded messages though his broadcasts out of Germany in a series of punctuated coughs, pauses, and the like, delivering important intelligence to the Allies. Though Nazis had been among his close friends and patrons as a playwright, Campbell romantically believes he can avoid politics before the war, even dreaming up a play about him and his wife called *Das Reich der Zwei—Nation of Two*—about "how a pair of lovers in a world gone mad could survive by being loyal only to a nation composed of themselves" (37). Campbell only assumes the views of a Nazi after he is asked by a Major from the United States War Department to work as an agent. He resists at first, but the Major wins him over with talk of good and evil, pure hearts and heroes. Campbell agrees, but his true motives are telling:

> He didn't mention the best reason for expecting me to go on and be a spy. The best reason was that I was a ham. As a spy of the sort he described, I would have an opportunity for some pretty grand acting. I would fool everyone with my brilliant interpretation of a Nazi, inside and out. (41)

In line with Vonnegut's admonition in the 1966 introduction to *Mother Night*, "we are what we pretend to be, so we must be careful what we pretend to be," Campbell's decision to play Nazi sets up the central question in the novel: Is Campbell a good guy or a bad guy? His work for the Allies would save him from the gallows after the war, but what is he *really*: an American hero or a Nazi propagandist? Through Campbell's ambiguous moral status, Vonnegut is asking more broadly where our authentic identities may be when we assume any sort of fiction for ourselves.

Vonnegut uses the vantage point of the double agent in his first novel to show sides of the story invisible to other characters. In *Mother Night*, the double agent device does that and then some. Practically everyone is working under double identities in the novel, which shows that the double self "is a device of survival much more in use at the present time than we realize" (Tanner 302). This functional schizophrenia among so many characters makes universal Vonnegut's notion that people tend to create fictions for themselves, one he explores often in later works.

Vonnegut further examines the role of the writer in *Mother Night*. As Tanner points out, "it is part of Vonnegut's meaning to suggest that the artist cannot rest confidently in the harmlessness of his inventions" (303). Certainly Vonnegut understood the similarities between public relations writing and propaganda; his comments on the function of writers as agents of social change (*Conversations* 76) underscore the level of responsibility he assigns to Campbell in *Mother Night*. But moreover, the fallibility of communication itself suggested in the novel by the (mis)use of various texts indicates early elements of postmodernism in Vonnegut's writing. The prevalence of black humor, and the act of stepping into the work himself (as he would in the introduction to the hardcover edition) aligns him with his postmodernist contemporaries.

Vonnegut's notions of fate and chance—along with his upbringing in a tight-knit German-American family so conscious of its origins—dictate much of the affinity between himself and Campbell in *Mother Night*. In the introduction he writes: "If I'd been born in Germany, I suppose I would have been a Nazi, bopping Jews and gypsies and Poles around, leaving boots sticking out of snowbanks, warming myself with my secretly virtuous insides" (*Mother Night* vii). Campbell's implied suicide at the novel's conclusion, too, originates with Vonnegut's mother's suicide in 1944; Vonnegut has said that it weighs heavily on his mind, as it must for all children of suicides, and it is telling that "Campbell's earlier attempt to escape into art is, in retrospect, made to appear rather equivocal" (Tanner 303).

The 1966 introduction marks Vonnegut's first description of his experiences in Dresden in print, and with much of *Mother Night* taking place in World War II Germany, we may presume that at this time Vonnegut is nearly ready to set down his war story in *Slaughterhouse-Five*. But while *Mother Night* may have prepared Vonnegut for *Slaughterhouse-Five* thematically, it is the brave, experimental narration of his next novel, *Cat's Cradle*, that would supply him with the style to tell *Slaughterhouse-Five* so effectively.

CHAPTER THREE

Call Me Jonah

> *Our society seems to engender a cadre of*
> *wonderfully motivated people who want earnestly to*
> *take charge and get things done. Conversely, I*
> *understand that in Paper Utopias like Cuba, people*
> *continually manage to forget to grease the trucks or*
> *get into the fields on time. What they obviously need*
> *is a more generous serving of the type of nuts we*
> *turn our enterprises over to—or who claw their way*
> *into control of them.*
>
> —Kurt Vonnegut, *Conversations*

IN THE 1960S, THINGS BEGAN to look up for Kurt Vonnegut. *Mother Night* appeared in paperback in 1962, though it carried a copyright date of 1961, and *Canary in a Cat House* was released in paperback that same year, reprinting many of Vonnegut's short stories written for magazines in the fifties. *The Sirens of Titan* was reissued in hardback in 1961, too, becoming Vonnegut's first novel printed in hardcover. Still, the declining short story market that first went sour in the late fifties proved to never recover, and Vonnegut's once lucrative short story career became non-existent. Publishing just three short stories in 1961, only two in 1962, and one in 1963, Vonnegut's financial situation became dire. He wrote *Cat's Cradle* to another paperback contract, and it was published in 1963.

CAT'S CRADLE

If *Slaughterhouse-Five* is Vonnegut's masterpiece, *Cats Cradle* is a close runner-up. One can see Vonnegut getting it right: the tight, focused satire of *Player Piano* reconciled with epic humor and odyssey of *The Sirens of Titan*, told effectively in the first person by a narrator who joins the action as the story progresses. It is a bitterly funny book, but one that captures Vonnegut's pessimism, his derision toward mankind—and its tendency to self-destruct— more than any of his novels before. Still, it received little critical attention, never outselling the original 6,000 copy print run; it would not be appreciated at the level it deserved until *Slaughterhouse-Five* forced critics back to his earlier works.

Cat's Cradle is doubtlessly informed by Vonnegut's truncated master's work in anthropology at the University of Chicago. While his thesis, "Fluctuations of Good and Evil in Simple Tales," which consisted of graphing the "shape" of popular story plots as diverse as Native American creation myths, fairy tales like Cinderella, and the narratives of the Bible, was unanimously rejected by the Anthropology Department in 1947, Vonnegut came away with a sense of cultural relativism, accepting all cultures and their belief systems as equally valid. Chicago's anthropology department in the forties was imbided with this way of thinking. Vonnegut explains, "Religions were exhibited and studied as the Rube Goldberg inventions I'd always though they were. We weren't allowed to find one culture superior to any other" (Hayman et al. 81). Besides "confirming his atheism," it freed Vonnegut to comment on American belief systems by creating his own, most explicitly, Bokononism in *Cat's Cradle*, The Church of Jesus Christ the Kidnapped in *Slapstick*, and the Church of God the Utterly Indifferent in *The Sirens of Titan*. In James Whitlark's analysis of Vonnegut's use and contributions to anthropology, he claims that cultural relativism allows the writer to create by "juxtapos[ing] patterns from many societies against science fiction 'alternatives to our society.'" This allows him to use old plots and still make a new statement on society (Whitlark 4).

More than humorous tropes in Vonnegut's fiction, these contrived belief systems are at the heart of his satirical process. In *Cat's Cradle,* one of the "old plots" is that of the Cinderella story. Here, the character experiences successive escalations of status: Cinderella is systematically raised by gift upon gift culminating in meeting the prince at the ball; the narrator of *Cat's Cradle* rises to become President of the pseudo-paradise of San Lorenzo and takes Mona, the most beautiful women on the island as his wife. But where Cinderella is tragically reverted to a plain-clothed peasant at the stroke of midnight *and then redeemed* by the true love of the prince, the narrator of *Cat's Cradle* is robbed of everything, and, since all life on earth is destroyed, redemption is impossible. The "new statement" is that belief systems of any kind are contrivances, and that nothing—not even love—is capable of bringing about salvation. Vonnegut's master's work comparing tales showed that Cinderella's rise, fall at the stroke of midnight, and re-escalation is identical to the Biblical fall and "rise to bliss ... with the expectation of redemption as expressed in primitive Christianity" (*Palm Sunday* 315). *Cat's Cradle* denies the possibility of any redemption, Christian, Bokononist, or otherwise. His version of the Cinderella story excludes the happy ending.

The narrator of *Cat's Cradle,* who says in the first lines of the book that his name is John but it might as well be Jonah, is introduced as a freelance writer who sets out to write a book called *The Day the World Ended.* Concerning the dawn of the atomic age, "[i]ts contents will be limited to events that took place on August 6, 1945, the day the bomb was dropped on Hiroshima" (*Cat's Cradle* 14). But while researching one apocalypse, Jonah/John witnesses another, becoming the last living thing on an earth destroyed by a compound called ice-nine that, by a complicated series of accidents, crystallizes all of the water on earth.

Even in the first pages of the book, an affinity between the narrator and Vonnegut himself is evident. Jonah and Vonnegut share the same profession, and belong to the same chapter of the same fraternity. The connection was originally conceived to be even more patent: Vonnegut "toyed with the idea of having his narrator find the Vonnegut name on an old tombstone," but, since readers would know that the tombstone bears the narrator's last name, too, "editors talked Vonnegut out of the idea as being too radical" (Klinkowitz, *Vonnegut in Fact* 111).

Jonah's search for material for *The Day the World Ended* leads him to contact Newt Hoenikker, son of the late Dr. Felix Hoenikker, one of the "fathers" of the atomic bomb. Hoenikker serves Vonnegut as a symbol of scientific irresponsibility, a man so withdrawn from humanity and so focused on childish play with nature that he has no perspective on the effects of his creations, and a total apathy for their uses. In Hoenikker, Vonnegut vilifies the moral irresponsibility of scientists he first witnessed in the research labs of General Electric. Vonnegut says in his 1973 *Playboy* interview that General Electric scientists "were all innocent, all simply dealing with truth and not worried about what might be done with their discoveries.... But [now] they've learned that anything they turn up will be applied if it can be. It's a law of life that if you turn up something that *can* be used violently, it *will* be used violently," (*Conversations* 97). Over the course of the novel we find that in his playfulness, Dr. Hoenikker created a substance even more pernicious than the atomic bomb, called ice-nine. Developed for the Marines to assuage, of all things, mud, ice-nine crystallizes water at room temperature. Hoenikker develops the substance in secret, "his last batch of brownies" (42) before he dies, and his children divide the tiny chip among the three of them. They all, in time, trade their pieces of this compound that would turn all the rivers, oceans, rain, people—anything containing water—into solid ice, in exchange for what they perceive to be love. Clearly, the Hoenikker children are trying to obtain something they were never able to get from their distant father.

Hoenikker's character is admittedly based on real-life General Electric scientist and Nobel Prize winner Irving Langmuir, described as "childlike in social relationships and claimed that he was simply unearthing the truth, that the truth could never hurt human beings and that he wasn't interested in the application of whatever he turned up" (*Conversations* 97). Vonnegut recalls in his "self-interview" that Langmuir is even responsible for some of Hoenikker's more endearing examples of absent-mindedness, and the origin of the concept of ice-nine:

> [Langmuir] wondered out loud one time whether, when turtles pulled in their heads, their spines buckled or contracted. I put that in the book. One time he left a tip under his plate after his wife served him breakfast at home. I put that in. His most important contribution, though, was the idea for what I called "Ice-9," a form of frozen water that was stable at room temperature. He didn't tell it directly to me. It was a legend around the laboratory—about the time H.G. Wells came to Schenectady.... Langmuir was told to be his host. Langmuir thought he might entertain Wells with an idea for a science-fiction story—about a form of ice that was stable at room temperature. Wells was uninterested, or at least never used the idea. And then Wells died, and then, finally, Langmuir died. I though to myself: "Finders, keepers—the idea is mine." (Hayman et al. 83)

But for the extensive portrayal of Hoenikker's absent mind and absent humanity—one character wonders if Dr. Hoenikker "wasn't born dead," saying he "never met a man less interested in living" (*Cat's Cradle* 53)—Hoenikker, whose discoveries brought about two apocalypses, one local and the other global, is presented with such adolescent qualities that his culpability is dubious at best. This is a Vonnegutian hallmark: there are never villains in his stories (*Fates Worse Than Death* 31).

Jonah follows the three Hoenikker children to the fictional island of San Lorenzo, a poor, desolate anti-paradise, "as unproductive as an equal area in the Sahara or the Polar Icecap," with "as dense a population as could be found anywhere, India and China not excluded" (*Cat's Cradle* 94). San Lorenzo was so worthless, we are told, that when a marine deserter named Corporal Earl McCabe and a hapless wandering Episcopalian named Lionel Boyd Johnson wash up like flotsam on its shores in 1922 and announced that they are taking control, no one seems to mind. In an effort to make San Lorenzo a Utopia, Johnson created a new religion, Bokononism, so named because of the pronunciation of "Johnson" in the inscrutable dialect of San Lorenzo. Vonnegut's ingenious use of metafictional techniques in *Cat's Cradle* has quotations from the Books of Bokonon and his Calypsos throughout the novel, becoming in the end a holy book itself.

Johnson/Bokonon described his motivations in one of his Calypsos:

> I wanted all things
> To seem to make some sense,
> So we could all be happy, yes,
> Instead of tense.
> And I made up lies
> So that they all fit nice,
> And I made this sad world
> A par-a-dise. (90)

Complete with its own lexicon, Bokononism stands as one of Vonnegut's most ingenious fictions. The lies in the song above are called *foma*, defined as harmless untruths, and if there is one basic tenet of this religion it is *Cat's Cradle's* epigraph, "live by the *foma* that make you brave and kind and healthy and happy" (4). Bokononism, like all religions, is intended to give people a sense of purpose, and for the wretched San Lorenzeans, the truth was so terrible that "Bokonon made it his business to provide the people with better and better lies." Faith, Vonnegut is pointing out, is based precisely on that which we do not know to be true, and this bears nothing on its efficacy. We are warned of this rather pessimistic message from the narrator early in the novel: "Anyone unable to understand how a useful religion can be founded on lies will not understand this book either" (14).

Bokonon realized that in order to make himself and his new religion attractive, he had to be seen against something more diabolical. So he asked McCabe to outlaw him and his religion. Bokonon's persecution and perceived ability to "miraculously" escape McCabe's manhunts made Bokononism immensely popular, though it was outlawed, directly boosting the happiness of the people. But, as in *Mother Night*, where people have a tendency to become the fictions they create for themselves, Johnson/Bokonon grows more insane in his role as "the gentle holy man in the jungle," and McCabe likewise as "the cruel tyrant in the city" (119).

Like Rumfoord in *The Sirens of Titan*, Vonnegut's message through Bokononism traces the futility of looking for purpose in events. Bokononism holds that "humanity is organized into teams, teams that do God's Will without ever discovering what they are doing" (11). He calls this group a *karass*. (Vonnegut took the name from the mailbox of his Cape Cod neighbor, whom he has never met—it is Greek.) But even as these teams unwittingly do what God wants them to, any effort to discern the purpose of the *karass* is futile. Any effort to discern the purpose of anything is futile. Bokonon demonstrates in a parable of sorts:

> I once knew an Episcopalian lady in Newport, Rhode Island, who asked me to design and build a doghouse for her Great Dane. The lady claimed to understand God and His Ways of Working perfectly. She could not understand why anyone should be puzzled about what had been or about what was going to be.
>
> And yet, when I showed her a blueprint of the doghouse I proposed to build, she said to me, "I'm sorry, but I never could read one of those things."
>
> "Give it to your husband or your minister to pass it on to God," I said, "and, when God finds a minute, I'm sure he'll explain this doghouse of mine in a way that even you could understand."
>
> She fired me. I shall never forget her. She believed that God liked people in sailboats much better than He liked people in motorboats. She could not bear to look at a worm. When she saw a worm, she screamed.
>
> She was a fool, and so am I, and so is anyone who thinks he sees what God is Doing, [writes Bokonon]. (13)

The *foma* in the idea of a *karass* is that the group is doing God's

Will, which cannot be known. "Nowhere does Bokonon warn against a person's trying to discover the limits of their *karass* and the nature of the work God Almighty has had it do," the narrator says. "Bokonon simply observes that such investigations are bound to be incomplete" (12–13). Everything is meant to happen, and we cannot know why. Attributing events or circumstances to God, though, "makes you brave and kind and healthy and happy." This Bokononist notion that things happen because they happen—stripped of any ostensible causality—foreshadows Billy Pilgrim's message in *Slaughterhouse-Five*.

Jonah's *karass* materializes on San Lorenzo. Frank, the oldest of Dr. Hoenikker's offspring, has traded his piece of ice-nine for a position in the island's government. Its dictator, Papa Monzano, sees the substance as a great way to blackmail foreign powers, and makes Frank a Major General. Monzano is dying of cancer, and Franklin Hoenikker is too shy to fulfill Monzano's wish that he be the next President. Frank puts Jonah up to it, and Jonah is swayed only when he discovers that he will get to marry the island's beautiful poster-girl, Mona Aamons. Trying to avoid his slow, painful death by cancer, Monzano swallows a chip of ice-nine, and is frozen solid. By chance (like everything else in the novel), a wayward plane from a patriotic display put on by San Lorenzo's Air Force crashes into Monzano's palace before his body can be disposed of. When it falls into the sea, the water of the world freezes solid.

"Call me Jonah" (11), reads the first sentence of *Cat's Cradle*. Here are two allusions simultaneously. For one, the line echoes the famous first line of Melville's *Moby Dick,* who's narrator, Ishmael, becomes the only survivor of Ahab's maddened quest for the great whale. Just as Ishmael relates the incomprehensibility of Ahab's voyage—and by extension, the incomprehensibility of the universe—Jonah becomes the last person on earth, and tells his own message of the inscrutable workings of the universe. Rich, also, is Vonnegut's allusion to the Hebrew book of Jonah. Jonah's reaction to God's call to prophecy has him run away from the city he is supposed to prophecy to, Nineveh, jump ship to Tarshish, be thrown into the sea by the ship's crew in a storm, and spend three days in the belly of a fish. God delivers Jonah from the fish, and this time, Jonah does go into Nineveh. The city is converted entirely. Because of this, God appears to Jonah to be unreliable: "When God saw what they did, how they turned from their evil ways, God changed his mind about the calamity that he had said he would bring upon them; and he did not do it" (Jonah 3:10). Jonah, in fact, wishes for his own death rather than grapple with the notion of an absolute God who can reverse his own perfect proclamations. In the Jonah story, Vonnegut finds God's compassion and ineffability at loggerheads, and it is that theology, that God's intentions are at all times unpredictable, that he incorporates into the Bokononism of *Cat's Cradle*.

Giannone's treatment of the use of the biblical tale of Jonah in *Cat's Cradle* takes Vonnegut's intentions even further. The Book of Jonah is idiosyncratic in the Hebrew Bible. Unlike other prophetical books, Jonah contains not oracles and admonitions about the wickedness of Israel and other nations, but is instead a narrative about the prophet himself, and it *shows* Jonah saving the town of Nineveh through preaching—it *shows* the prophet in action; it *shows* the people of Nineveh changing their ways. "Vonnegut implies through his novelistic use of Jonah that science has led us so far astray that the enormous cry of Old Testament prophecy is needed to correct the course of life" (Giannone 56). It is the preaching, the form of this novel—unique as the book of Jonah is unique—that is capable of deliverance.

Cat's Cradle is indeed a new form of the novel itself. Allen notes that Vonnegut's massive paperback audience, earned through the genre fiction of *Player Piano, The Sirens of Titan,* and *Mother Night,* allowed him to teach "a new generation of readers"—the college crowd that would bring him to the attention of the Academy—"how to perceive fiction in a new way" (*Understanding Kurt Vonnegut* 55). The "willing suspension of disbelief," the traditional theory of fiction from Coleridge to the present, is exchanged for the book's epigraph "Nothing in this book is true" (*Cat's Cradle* 4), and Bokonon's "All of the true things I am about to tell you are shameless lies" (14). Such meta-fictional techniques, where the artist calls attention to his own artifice, would be embraced by this new generation, ushering in what is called postmodernist fiction.

Cat's Cradle may well be Vonnegut's most pessimistic book up until this point. Its blatant account of the failure of science and religion to circumvent human suffering leaves little hope for humanity. Even love—the love between Jonah and Mona—fails to provide a reason to stay alive.

GOD BLESS YOU, MR. ROSEWATER

The link between mental health and economics is present in much of Vonnegut's fiction, by the example of his parents. The Liebers, Vonnegut's mother's family, had made a fortune operating a brewery in Indianapolis, and her wedding to the young second-generation architect, third-generation American Kurt Vonnegut Sr. was one of the most extravagant affairs Indianapolis had ever seen. Prohibition meant the end of the Lieber brewery, but the Vonneguts lived well on an architect's income, affording private school for Kurt Jr.'s two older siblings, and the private Orchard School for Vonnegut until 1936. But by then the family's fortune had subsided to the point that Kurt had to attend public high school. The depreciation of wealth and status proved too much for Vonnegut's mother, who suffered from mental illness for years, eventually committing suicide by an overdose of sleeping pills after her youngest son went to war. Kurt Sr. took the economic decline more spiritually, losing a sense of purpose as he failed to receive a commission for years after the stock market crash of 1929. This relationship between sanity and dignity is especially potent in *God Bless You, Mr. Rosewater.*

The protagonist in the novel is Eliot Rosewater, heir to the Rosewater fortune and President of the Rosewater Foundation, its philanthropic arm. Eliot's sanity is called into question by his endless drinking, frequent wanderings, and finally his decision to return to the family home in Rosewater, Indiana, where he devotes the Rosewater fortune's charities to the people of Rosewater County. Much of the evidence for Rosewater's mental degradation we see through the eyes of Norman Mushari—as close to a villain as Vonnegut comes to writing—a young lawyer with the firm that handles the Rosewater fortune. Mushari uses his privy to Rosewater documents to see the fortune change hands, setting up Fred Rosewater, a distant cousin, as heir, intending to take a chunk of the vast sum along the way.

Maddened Eliot disappears from his sophisticated wife early in the novel, reappearing in various parts of the country. He shows up drunk at a science fiction writer's convention in Pennsylvania. His address to the crowd is Vonnegut's defense of his craft:

> I love you sons of bitches…. You're all I read anymore. You're the only ones who'll talk about the really terrific changes going on, the only ones crazy enough to know that life is a space voyage, and not a short one, either, but one that'll last for billions of years. You're the only ones with guts enough to really care about the future, who really notice what machines do to us, what wars do to us, what cities do to us, what big, simple ideas do to us, what tremendous misunderstandings, mistakes, accidents and catastrophes do to us. You're the only ones zany enough to agonize over time and distances without limit, over mysteries that will never die, over the fact that we are right now determining whether the space voyage for the next billion years or so is going to be Heaven or Hell. (*God Bless You, Mr. Rosewater* 18)

Eliot surfaces, too, at volunteer fire departments around the country, genuinely trying to help out and making suggestions for more effective firefighting. After a time, he winds up in ancestral Rosewater County, seat of his family homestead, though his father's Senatorial duties have severed any ties to the place. What Eliot sees convinces him of his vocation. "I look at these people, these Americans," Eliot tells his wife when first landing in Rosewater, "and I realize that they can't even care about themselves anymore—because they have no *use*. The factory, the farms, the mine across the river—they're almost completely automatic now" (36). Like the populace on Homestead in *Player Piano*, the majority of people living in Rosewater County were put out of work by automation, and a sense of uselessness ensued. As an architect, Vonnegut's father did not lose his job to automation, but his eleven years without a commission during the Great Depression ushered in a lack of purpose. This lack of dignity stemming from feelings of economic uselessness is extant again and again in Vonnegut's fiction. Eliot's solution: "I'm going to love these discarded Americans, even though they're useless and unattractive. That is going to be my work of art" (36). He moves the headquarters of the Rosewater Foundation to Rosewater, and goes about the business of loving its people.

Edith Vonnegut's reaction to her family's financial misfortune is probably best portrayed in the behavior of the Rosewater cousin, Fred, a middle-class insurance salesman surrounded by Rhode Island old money. Fred longs for excitement in his life, and his marriage suffers from his wife's unhappiness in the middle class. Caroline Rosewater is embarrassed for what little money Fred takes home, especially in comparison to her neighbors' New England wealth, and she would be happy only in a life like that of her friend, Amanita Buntline—one where she might, for instance, spend $17 on a toilet paper cover without a thought. Fred wanders about his days trying to scare the working class into life insurance policies to establish a "fortune" for their families should they die. His depression is so bad that he is thinking of ways to kill himself the afternoon we meet him. "Sons of suicides often think of killing themselves at the end of the day," we are told, "when their blood sugar is low" (138). Fred and others in the novel are in fact always at the brink of suicide, regardless of their particular caste, but always regarding money—reminiscent of Vonnegut's own mother's mental collapse and eventual suicide, stemming ultimately from her family's inability to remain in the upper class.

That suicide seems always imminent, always a possibility, is paralleled in Eliot Rosewater's view that earth's oxygenated atmosphere "was eager to combine violently with almost every-thing [earth's] inhabitants held dear" (22). This grim view that things are forever on the brink of destruction has been noticed by critic Clark Mayo: "the world of Vonnegut's fiction is ... constantly under the threat of annihilation" (Mayo 26). Eliot's mania for fire and fire prevention is due to his accidental slaying of several firefighters when he mistook them for S.S. men during his service in the war, who were trying to extinguish a clarinet factory. On this account he is, like Howard W. Campbell Jr. and many of Vonnegut's future characters, a guilt-ridden protagonist trying to reconcile himself with his past. Giannone points out that Eliot's guilt is his prime motive for taking the Rosewater Foundation to task. Eliot:

> lays his life down before the troubles of others. The guilt lingers. To try to make amends, he becomes the spiritual volunteer fireman in Rosewater, ready to answer every human emergency that comes through his black phone (which is near the red phone he answers as Fire Lieutenant). Eliot takes on the crimes of his personal and familial past along with the disasters that are the world's estate. (Giannone 74)

In time, Mushari approaches Fred Rosewater (literally right before he hangs himself), and Eliot's sanity will be on trial. On one of Eliot's catatonic utterances, his nervous father, the Senator, brings Kilgore Trout, the washed-up science fiction writer of dozens of cheap, garish, outlandish books to help with the case. Trout is recognizable throughout Vonnegut's novels as his surrogate, his alter-ego, in that he is what Vonnegut feared he himself could be, the writer of countless unread, superficial science fiction novels with a statement that nobody gets, being made to take bad jobs to support his writing. (Here he works at a stamp redemption center. In *Slaughterhouse-Five*, he supervises unreliable boys selling magazine subscriptions.) He is Vonnegut's mouthpiece declaring that Eliot is in fact not insane, that his work with the Rosewater Foundation "was quite possibly the most import social experiment of our time, for it dealt on a very small scale with a problem whose queasy horrors will eventually be made world-wide by the sophistication of machines. The problem is this: How to love people who have no use?" (*God Bless You, Mr. Rosewater* 183).

Eliot's Barry Goldwateresque, Joe McCarthyesque, moral-legislating father, Senator Rosewater, fails to see that Trout is in fact giving perfectly sensible reasons for Eliot's sanity, and instead thinks it only a good defense in court. But this is precisely the socioeconomic dilemma that Vonnegut is exposing in the novel, and Trout demonstrates the matter succinctly. Vonnegut's socialist views inform much of the novel's message. Asked by his father if he is a communist, Eliot replies,

> [N]obody can work with the poor and not fall over Karl Marx from time to time—or just fall over the Bible, as far as that goes. I think it's terrible the way people don't share things in this country. I think it's a heartless government that will let one baby be born owning a big piece of the country, the way I was born, and let another baby be born without owning anything. The least a government could do, it seems to me, is to divide things up fairly among the babies. Life is hard enough, without people having to worry themselves sick about *money*, too. There's plenty for everybody in this country, if we'll only just *share* more. (87–88)

Though seeming rather progressive from our current, post-Reagan perspective, Vonnegut was certainly not alone espousing this viewpoint in the mid-sixties. The "War on Poverty" and Great Society of the Kennedy-Johnson administrations were still well underway. Rather than suggesting that such a mentality be engendered in America, *God Bless You, Mr. Rosewater* is Vonnegut lauding the current political climate, and debunking the Goldwater right who sought the acquiescence of government involvement in socioeconomics in the 1964 presidential election. (Senator Rosewater, incidentally, is yet another of Vonnegut's "historical" figures, as Rumfoord of *The Sirens of Titan* is a caricature of Franklin Roosevelt, or Dan Gregory is Norman Rockwell in *Bluebeard*.)

The resolution has Eliot adopting the dozens of children women have accused him of fathering in Rosewater County, thus making Fred Rosewater's relation too distant to make a claim on the Rosewater fortune, regardless of Eliot's mental status. It is Eliot's ultimate act of unconditional love towards others. The distribution of Eliot's fortune makes things fair, but it is not necessarily monetary altruism that Vonnegut advocates; emotional altruism is what is prescribed for humanity. Trout suggests volunteer fire departments are an appropriate model (note that Vonnegut has long been active in fire departments, and that this was written decades before the September 11 attacks):

> "[T]hey are, when the alarm goes off, almost the only examples of enthusiastic unselfishness to be seen in this land. They rush to the rescue of any human being, and count not the cost. The most contemptible man in town, should his contemptible house catch fire, will see his enemies put the fire out. And, as he pokes through the ashes for the remains of his contemptible possessions, he will be comforted and pitied by no less than the Fire Chief."
>
> Trout spread his hands. "There we have people treasuring people as people. It's extremely rare. So from this we must learn." (*God Bless You, Mr. Rosewater* 184)

God Bless You, Mr. Rosewater was finally granted critical review after its publication, though it seems to lack much of the style and jazz that Vonnegut seemed to be working toward in his first four novels. But Peter Reed cautions against discounting the novel in its apparently traditional form:

> Compared with [*Cat's Cradle* and *Slaughterhouse-Five*], Rosewater appears to be a reconventionalized novel, shorn of the experimentation with language, fragmentation, narration-within-narration, and self-reflexive fictionality that are their hallmarks. Yet while it returns to the novel's traditional preoccupations with money and social morality, it does so in a manner appropriate to its own era, and it is not without elements of the innovation that so characterizes the other two books. (Merrill 109).

Reed goes on to cite the novel's latent and manifest intertextuality with *Hamlet,* its frequent throwbacks to family histories as reasons for many of the predicaments in the book, Trout's and Eliot's use of fictions to rationalize Eliot's sanity, among other things, as perfect examples of metafiction working in Rosewater. The novel was nonetheless a departure from the experimental breakthrough that was *Cat's Cradle,* and despite its heavy print runs and sales, it received mediocre reviews. Martin Levin's critique in the *New York Times* called Vonnegut's visions "less flamboyant" and his narrative "less inventive" than *Cat's Cradle*, saying that *Rosewater* is more a series of random meditations than a work of fiction. (April 25, 1965)

Rosewater was Vonnegut's only novel in print by 1965. Mostly to support his family, Vonnegut accepted a teaching position at the University of Iowa's Writer's Workshop that same year. Though his decision to take the post in Iowa was underwritten by purely pragmatic, financial reasons, it would prove to be a major turning point in his career, and not coincidentally. Until then, Vonnegut had been living a sequestered literary life in Cape Cod, and so feedback and association with what other writers were doing at the time was rare for him. At Iowa, he finally talked with other writers, scholars, and creatively inclined students, who advocated, or at least supported, a view of the way books ought to be written that was not wholly representational. The spirit in which Vonnegut penned *Cat's Cradle* was not only acceptable, he found, but moreover a valid means of expression. When Eliot reaches the pinnacle of his insanity, he envisions Indianapolis enveloped in a great firestorm. The hallucination is inspired by a book he read about the destruction of Dresden; its appearance and description in *God Bless You Mr. Rosewater* marks Vonnegut's readiness to approach his own Dresden experience in his writing. For years he had been trying to say what he needed to say about Dresden, and after Iowa, he found a voice.

CHAPTER FOUR

So It Goes

Time warps, spaceships, and galactic materializations aside, Vonnegut, an earthling like all of us, can not push his vision past the ironic barrier of the mind. He bestows on his ideal creatures, the Tralfamadorians, the supreme privilege of blowing up the universe. They blow it up, of all things, experimenting with a new fuel for flying saucers. So much, then, for Universal Time and Space, where vision and extinction finally become one.

—Ihab Hassan, *Liberations*

SLAUGHTERHOUSE-FIVE

That seventeen years went by from the time Vonnegut published his first novel to the appearance of *Slaughterhouse-Five* is evidence enough that Vonnegut had work to do before he could address his experiences in Dresden. The Writers Workshop at Iowa was pivotal, to be sure, in allowing Vonnegut to find a voice in which he may tell the story. In 1967, he was awarded a Guggenheim Fellowship which allowed him time to travel to Dresden to research the novel. The windfall of his three-book-deal with

Seymour Lawrence, recorded charmingly in *Slaughterhouse-Five* itself (18), gave Vonnegut the time and money necessary to begin devoting himself to his Dresden book whole-heartedly. The dreamy circumstances surrounding Vonnegut's collaboration with Sam Lawrence are detailed by Vonnegut friend and fellow author Dan Wakefield in the *Vonnegut Statement*. Wakefield claims to have it from Sam himself that he contacted Vonnegut after reading his notorious review of the new Random House dictionary in the *New York Times*, October 30, 1966. Actually, this short, funny piece on Random House's latest effort would not just attract the attention of a publisher willing to sign an author to three books and pay a sum of Vonnegut's choosing in advance of royalties. It has been postulated that one reason Vonnegut managed to go from the cloistered audience of college science fiction readers to the front page of the *New York Times Book Review* was precisely his work for that publication, "New Dictionary" included. Vonnegut dropped by Lawrence's Boston office one day, "[a]nd it all began, the very nice relationship of Vonnegut as author and Sam as his publisher" (Klinkowitz, *The Vonnegut Statement* 65).

Vonnegut was a battalion scout in the 106th infantry, which arrived on the European front in November of 1944. The Battle of the Bulge, the last tremendous German effort on the Western front, caught the Allies in the Ardennes of Belgium in mid-December, and Vonnegut became a prisoner of war. He and others were sent first to a camp south of Dresden and later moved into Dresden proper, and put to work in a factory that made vitamin supplements for pregnant women. Dresden was not an open city, contrary to some publications over the years, but it is true that Axis military presence in the area was small, that the city had not been a target yet in the war, and that with the war winding down, no one expected to be bombed. It was nevertheless decimated by Allied aircraft on the night of February 13–14, 1945, where a firestorm was created by dropping incendiaries followed by saturation bombing. Some reports have it that the surface temperature in Dresden reached over 2000°F. Civilian deaths have been estimated between 35,000 and 135,000. Vonnegut became one of very few people to survive the event, taking shelter along with a few dozen other American POW's and their German guards in an underground meat locker called *Slaughterhouse-Five*, in the warehouse district where they were imprisoned.

The author recalls that he considered writing what he had seen soon after it was over. Little had been mentioned about the firebombing in American newspapers, however, and it wasn't until he met and spoke with Europeans that he realized his Dresden experience was something truly unique after all. He and other soldiers were amazed that the Allies were engaged in the destruction of civilian cities, but as a 22-year-old private in 1945, Vonnegut had no way of judging the extent of the catastrophe or questioning the Allies' reasons for doing it. Reliable figures of casualties had not been available after the war. It was only when he began to research the raid, writing to the Air Force, for one, that he found much of the information about the firebombing was classified. He began to question the motivations and consequences of warfare under the resistance he discovered in trying to obtain accurate information about Dresden. The reality of the event and government attempts to suppress this reality were eye-opening for the survivor; the duplicity of the American government was made plain in its gloss of what happened at Dresden:

> Our generation did believe what its Government said—because we weren't lied to very much. One reason we weren't lied to was that there wasn't a war going on in our childhood, and so essentially we were told the truth. There was no reason for our Government to lie very elaborately to us. But a government at war does become a lying government for many reasons. One reason is to confuse the enemy. When we went into the war, we felt our Government was a respecter of life, careful about not injuring civilians and that sort of thing. Well, Dresden had no tactical value; it was a city of civilians. Yet the Allies bombed it until it burned and melted. And then they lied about it. All that was startling to us. (*Conversations* 95)

As Allen puts it, the implications "came gradually, as a long process of thinking about the nature of war and writing about it, at first unsuccessfully" (*Understanding Kurt Vonnegut* 80). Finally, he arrived at the real story worth telling: not the raid itself, but all it implies, "to one man, to each individual man, to all men collectively" (Reed 173).

The trick is to somehow portray the events as they affected him and simultaneously show their significance to everyone else. At the same time, there must be some narrative distance allowing comment on what is portrayed. Crucially, Vonnegut is in the book. The first chapter details how he came to write the novel, and relates his difficulty in finding the words to express what happened at Dresden and what Dresden means; his presence authenticates his story in a way impossible otherwise. This augments a metafictional tendency marked first with his intrusion by way of introduction in the 1966 hardcover edition of *Mother Night,* although that innovation is worlds away from the altogether first-person frame of *Slaughterhouse.*

We find out that at least part of his difficulty is due to his poor memory of what happened, so he calls an old friend, Bernard V. O'Hare, who survived the bombing along with Vonnegut. As he tells the story in *Slaughterhouse-Five,* Vonnegut can't help but notice a certain animosity in Bernard's wife, Mary:

> Then she turned to me, let me see how angry she was, and that the anger was for me. She had been talking to herself, so what she said was a fragment of a much larger conversation. "You were just babies then!" she said.
>
> "What?" I said.
>
> "You were just babies in the war, like the ones upstairs!"
>
> I nodded that this was true. We had been foolish virgins in the war, right at the end of childhood.
>
> "But you're not going to write it that way, are you." This wasn't a question. It was an accusation.
>
> "I—I don't know," I said.
>
> "Well, I know," she said. "You'll pretend you were men instead of babies, and you'll be played in the movies by Frank Sinatra and John Wayne or some of those other glamorous, war-loving, dirty

old men. And war will look just wonderful, so we'll have a lot more of them. And they'll be fought by babies like the babies upstairs." (*Slaughterhouse-Five* 14)

Her real-life reaction to his project was "a very important clue" in helping Vonnegut discover what he wanted to say. "She freed me to write about what infants we really were: 17, 18, 19, 20, 21." (Hayman et al., 69). It is a first step in dictating the implications of war, instead of depicting the events of World War II alone. Vonnegut dedicates the book to Mary O'Hare (and to a taxi driver he and O'Hare befriended on their second trip to Germany). He addresses her concerns in the novel, in a passage that shows how her insight led to the straight-forward, unglamorous truth telling of *Slaughterhouse*:

So I held up my right hand and I made her a promise: "Mary," I said, "I don't think this book of mine is ever going to be finished. I must have written five thousand pages by now, and thrown them all away. If I ever do finish it, though, I give you my word of honor: there won't be a part for Frank Sinatra or John Wayne.
"I tell you what," I said, "I'll call it 'The Children's Crusade.'"
She was my friend after that. (*Slaughterhouse-Five* 15)

"The Children's Crusade" becomes one of the book's subtitles, a title which not only alludes to the unheroic age of the soldiers who fought the war, but to the original Children's Crusade of 1213, the story of which Vonnegut sets down in the first chapter, too. The inhumanity of raising an army of well-meaning and desperate children and subsequently shipping them not to Palestine but as slaves to North Africa is thus drawn as a parallel to Vonnegut's story of young men sent to fight, and the civilians—children among them—killed in the process.

Vonnegut achieves his distance by making the war and its aftermath happen to a fictional character, Billy Pilgrim. Vonnegut is there, we know; but he tells the story through Pilgrim as a way to make claims by example—a technique that would be impossible in a first person, autobiographical account. Because

Dresden happens to Pilgrim, who is apathetic, even unfazed by his wartime experiences, it provides Vonnegut with the tools to show one of the gravest malefactions of warfare: forgetting that it happened.

Vonnegut also calls the story a "Duty-dance with Death," and death and dying subsume the novel, marked everywhere with the Vonnegutian refrain, "so it goes." The tired weight of this repetition whenever anyone or anything dies in the book serves to remind the reader of death's everpresence, with each instance of the phrase heaving mortality in its utterance. The dance is the helter-skelter chronology of the book, which is due to Billy Pilgrim's having become "unstuck in time," having no control over the moment in life he is now attending. Pilgrim's story is told piecemeal as he jumps to times in his life before, during, and after the war, dancing with death all the while.

Pilgrim's war story is much like Vonnegut's. He gets lost in the confusion of the Battle of the Bulge almost immediately on his arrival, and wanders for days behind German lines with two scouts and an anti-tank gunner named Roland Weary. As a poorly-clothed, unarmed chaplain's assistant, Pilgrim is a liability to the others in the group—in dress shoes with a broken heel he has a hard time keeping up—and the professionalism of the two scouts puts him under the care of the despicable Weary, whose macabre sensibilities are evident in the considerable romance he ascribes to the business of war. Billy's handicaps lead the two scouts to desert Weary and himself, and Weary (who had imagined their little group as "The Three Musketeers") nearly beats the frozen, starving Pilgrim to death on this account. His assault is only halted by their capture by German soldiers. The Germans take away Weary's valuable combat boots; he develops gangrene on his feet and dies in a severely overcrowded train car days later, blaming Pilgrim out loud. The wiry Paul Lazzaro pledges to avenge Weary's death.

The trains finally arrive at a prison camp, where the Americans find themselves guests of well-appointed British officers who have been there since the war began. Due to a clerical error, they have been receiving ten times their allotted aid packages from the Red Cross, and have arranged a feast and a "musical version of Cinderella" (96) for the emaciated Americans. The feast makes everybody sick, including "the author of this book" who tells Billy he just excreted his brains (125). Shipped to Dresden shortly after, Billy (like Vonnegut) is put to work in a vitamin factory. He survives the firestorm with a hundred other American prisoners, their German guards, and the American Nazi propagandist Howard W. Campbell Jr. in a meat locker underneath a slaughterhouse. They are made to mine for corpses in the ruins.

After the war Billy suffers from a nervous breakdown while finishing his degree at the Ilium School of Optometry. While he is hospitalized he meets Eliot Rosewater, a huge fan of the novels of Kilgore Trout, who becomes Billy's favorite novelist, too. He marries the school founder's daughter, and makes a fortune selling frames to factory workers in town. He produces two children, and in 1967 is abducted by a flying saucer that takes him as a specimen for a zoo on the planet Tralfamadore. He is mated there with a porn star named Montana Wildhack and produces another child, but since he went through a time-warp to get there it does not take any years away form his earthly life.

The Tralfamadorians are the ultimate outsiders. Not only do they have the benefit of viewing earth from far away, but their ability to see in the fourth dimension lets them see all events in time at once. They know how the universe will end, just as they can see how a person will die, and it is their approach to the uncontrollable universe that Billy adopts as a way to cope with the tragedies and uncertainties of existence. A Tralfamadorian guide tells Pilgrim that the universe blows up when they experiment with new fuels for flying saucers:

"If you know this, said Billy, "isn't there some way you can prevent it? Can't you keep the pilot from *pressing* the button?"

"He has *always* pressed it, and he always *will*. We *always* let him and we always *will* let him. The moment is *structured* that way." (*Slaughterhouse-Five* 117)

The Tralfamadorians cope with this and all other terrible inevitabilities by not looking at them. It is a non-solution, of course, much like Billy's own complacency in the post-war period. "That's one thing Earthlings might learn to do, if they tried hard enough: Ignore the awful times, and concentrate on the good ones" (117).

In 1968 Pilgrim becomes the sole survivor of a plane crash. His wife, insane with concern, gets in a car accident on the way to the hospital that takes the exhaust from her Cadillac; she dies of carbon monoxide poisoning moments after she arrives at the hospital where Billy is infirmed. When Billy gets home he embraces the task of telling the world what he learned about time and life on Tralfamadore. He writes letters to newspapers and tries to get on talk shows. He foresees his own death in 1976, where he is to be assassinated speaking to a capacity crowd on the nature of time and flying saucers in a domed baseball stadium by a man hired by Paul Lazarro, who makes good on his word.

Vonnegut warns on the title page that the novel is told "somewhat in the schizophrenic telegraphic manner of the tales of the planet Tralfamadore," which accounts for the lack of chronology in the short scenes we see. Billy gets to see one of these Tralfamadorian novels in his travels. One of the aliens explains:

> [E]ach clump of symbols is a brief, urgent message—describing a situation, a scene. We Tralfamadorians read them all at once, not one after the other. There isn't any particular relationship between all the messages, except that the author has chosen them carefully so that, when seen all at once, they produce an image of life that is beautiful and surprising and deep. There is no beginning, no middle, no end, no causes, no effects. What we love in our books are the depths of many marvelous moments seen all at one time. (88)

Vonnegut tells his publisher in the first chapter that his novel "is so short and jumbled and jangled, Sam, because there is nothing intelligent to say about a massacre" (19). Because Vonnegut cannot find any good reason—any *cause* for Dresden, he finds himself narrating the circumstances of the event like a

Tralfamadorian. The extraordinary effect of this in the novel is to make all events, no matter *when* they occurred, to *lead up to* Dresden. Traditional cause and effect undergo utter evisceration. Reed shows how the structure of *Slaughterhouse-Five* works to achieve this through the Tralfamadorian model:

> Aside from the fact that the Tralfamadorians, in their novels as in their minds, emphasize beautiful moments and exclude the unpleasant ones, Slaughterhouse-Five almost fits their requirements. Most of the situations described are grim, many downright painful. The "clumps of symbols" obviously cannot be read simultaneously, either, but the way in which short scenes from several points in time are spliced together does help sustain the impression of concurrent actions, and intensifies the sense of an interrelationship of events transcending time. Nor is there always a "particular relationship between all the messages," but they often do show a kinship of theme or image, and they cohere to create "an image of life" which, while not always "beautiful," is frequently "surprising" and in total effect quite "deep." Because all of its scenes cannot be read simultaneously, the book comes closer to possessing a climax than does the Tralfamadorian novel. It is hard to single out one climactic event, be it the raid itself or the ironic execution of Edgar Derby, but the novel certainly builds towards the end where the meaning, the questions and the emotional impact come together. (Reed 179–180)

Besides making Dresden the inevitable consequence and influence of every event in the novel, the Tralfamadorian vision, which strips events of their identifiable reasons, presents a view of life unable to be anything but fatalist. One Tralfamadorian tells Billy that "All time is time. It does not change. It does not lend itself to warnings or explanations. It simply *is*" (*Slaughterhouse-Five* 86). The absence of will falls in place with the message Malachi Constant brings back to Earth at the behest of Rumfoord in *The Sirens of Titan*: "I was a victim of a series of accidents, as are we all" (*The Sirens of Titan* 229).

Vonnegut's nonlinear construction of time, however, does more than throw causality to the wind: it is in fact a way of replicating the human experience. Time travel is possible—through memory. Even if we cannot, like the Tralfamadorians, look at all different moments just the way Tralfamadorians can "look at a stretch of the Rocky Mountains" (*Slaughterhouse-Five* 27), we may still maintain a will to live by remembering only the "nice moments"—even in an uncertain and often painful cosmos. It is the Tralfamadorian way of life—to "forget" everything displeasing and "remember" only the "nice" moments.

That is, of course, precisely not what Vonnegut would have us do. "If what Billy Pilgrim learned from the Tralfamadorians is true, that we will all live forever, no matter how dead we may sometimes seem to be," Vonnegut writes in the tenth chapter, "I am not overjoyed. Still—if I am going to spend eternity visiting this moment and that, I'm grateful that so many of those moments are nice" (211). The author *has* looked back, remembering the countless deaths with the "so it goes" refrain. He claims in the first chapter that the book is a failure, because, like Lot's wife, he looked back at destruction (22). His closing point is that there is an awful lot of suffering in the world, and while he (and the reader) may have so many "nice moments" to remember, hundreds of thousands of others in the world do not. On the plane to Dresden with O'Hare, his old war buddy supplies him with population statistics that demonstrate this:

On an average, 324,000 new babies are born into the world each day. During that same day, 10,000 persons, on an average, will have starved to death or died from malnutrition. So it goes. In addition 123,000 persons will die for other reasons. So it goes. This leaves a net gain of about 191,000 people each day in the world. The Population Reference Bureau predicts that the world's total population will double to 7,000,000,000 before the year 2000.
"I suppose they will all want dignity," I said.
"I suppose," said O'Hare. (212)

His timing was impeccable. *Slaughterhouse-Five's* 1969 publication was embraced by his already energized college readers, who saw increasing American involvement in Vietnam just as nonsensical as Vonnegut presented his Dresden experience. His last chapter brings what has already been portrayed as a universally significant event right up to the present:

> Robert Kennedy, whose summer home is eight miles from the home I live in all year round, was shot two nights ago. He died last night. So it goes.
>
> Martin Luther King was shot a month ago. He died, too. So it goes.
>
> And everyday my Government gives me a count of corpses created by military science in Vietnam. So it goes. (210)

Of course, some readers were turned off by the superficial absurdity of the novel. Space aliens and time-travel and such are easy elements to seize upon in a charge of insipidity. Christopher Lehmann-Haupt's *Times* review praised the novel, but added that "it is also very Vonnegut, which means you'll either love it, or push it back in the science fiction corner," (March 31, 1969). David Standish of *Playboy* asked Vonnegut why, if the novel is about the firebombing of Dresden, would the novel be written in "science fiction mode." The answer to *Playboy* is a definitive comment on the fantastic in all his work:

> These things are intuitive. There's never any strategy meeting about what you're going to do; you just come to work everyday. And the science-fiction passages in *Slaughterhouse-Five* are just like the clowns in Shakespeare. When Shakespeare figured the audience had had enough of the heavy stuff, he'd let up a little, bring on a clown or a foolish innkeeper or something like that, before he'd become serious again. And trips to other planets, science fiction of an obviously kidding sort, is equivalent to bringing on the clowns every so often to lighten things up. (*Conversations* 94)

Especially since *Cat's Cradle*, it has been clear that Vonnegut will embrace experimental forms of storytelling to make his point.

The convoluted chronology of *Slaughterhouse-Five* is symptomatic of Vonnegut's view that old plots—especially "Western civilization's most enthusiastically received story," Cinderella (*Palm Sunday* 315), or, thanks to Vonnegut's graduate work in anthropology, the Judeo-Christian Bible's story of fall and redemption—have failed humanity. The novel calls attention to its Christian leitmotif no earlier than its epigraph:

> The cattle are lowing,
> The Baby awakes.
> But the little Lord Jesus
> No crying He makes.

Pilgrim is set up as a Christ figure in deed and description. Crucial to understanding Vonnegut's replacement of the story of Christ is the Kilgore Trout novel, *The Gospel From Outer Space,* in which an alien undertakes a study of Christianity, "to learn, if he could, why Christians found it so easy to be cruel." He concludes that, because of "slipshod storytelling in the New Testament," the message of mercy in the gospels has been misinterpreted to read: "*Before you kill somebody, make absolutely sure he isn't well connected.*" The alien infers that since people thought, "*Oh boy—they sure picked the wrong guy to lynch that time!*" it followed that, "*[t]here are right people to lynch*"—namely, the less connected (*Slaughterhouse-Five* 108–109). The alien's revision has Jesus as a bum and a nobody, who is adopted as the Son of the Creator of the Universe after his crucifixion with the pronouncement that "*From this moment on, He will punish horribly anybody who torments a bum who has no connections!*" Billy is the bum, of course, since he is Cinderella (145), and since Vonnegut tells us that the epigraph was chosen because both Billy and the Baby Jesus cry soundlessly.

Billy becomes aware of his own impending death but resolves to use it to teach people how to view death in the world. His message promises immortality:

> The most important thing I learned on Tralfamadore was that

when a person dies he only appears to die. He is still very much alive in the past, so it is very silly for people to cry at his funeral. (26–27)

Billy's words before his execution in Chicago are highly allusive to Christ's teachings. He tells his disciple-like audience that he will be killed very soon, and:

> There are protests from the crowd.
> Billy Pilgrim rebukes them. "If you protest, if you think that death is a terrible thing, then you will not have understood a word I've said."

And when police try to protect him from his fate:

> "No, no," says Billy serenely. "It is time for you to go home to your wives and children, and it is time for me to be dead for a little while—and then live again." At that moment, Billy's high forehead is in the cross hairs of a high-powered laser gun. It is aimed at him from the darkened press box. In the next moment, Billy Pilgrim is dead. So it goes.
> So Billy experiences death for a while. It is simply violet light and a hum. There isn't anybody else there. Not even Billy Pilgrim is there:
>> Then he swings back into life again, all the way back to an hour after his life was threatened by Lazzaro—in 1945. (142–143)

So while Christ teaches an everlasting life in Heaven or Hell, "Billy, the new Christ, preaches that human beings *do* have eternal life—even if there is no life after death" (*Understanding Kurt Vonnegut* 88). "The identification can be taken seriously if not solemnly," writes Reed, noting that Pilgrim's role as Christ is just one of the ways he is presented as an Everyman, a "universal man-child." "At times it becomes ludicrous—but that is exactly the point. Billy's being moonishly bemused, utterly helpless, even ridiculous, fits him for the role of persecuted child, of babe born to die" (185).

Vonnegut has created religions in his books in the past, and he would continue to do so in future novels, but none provoked such ire as *Slaughterhouse-Five*. The book was banned from several school districts' libraries and reading lists, and even burned in a few communities. "Acting on a teen-aged girl's complaint that Kurt Vonnegut's "*Slaughterhouse-Five*" was "profane," the school board of a town in North Dakota ordered all copies of the book burned, after a search of students' lockers to ascertain that they had harbored none of the dangerous contraband," the *New York Times* reported on November 17, 1973. "The board members were undoubtedly encouraged in their act of censorship by ministers who called the Vonnegut novel a "tool of the devil." This is indicative of most of the charges against the novel, that it was either "antireligious" (one judge in Detroit ruled that its presence on a suggested reading list violated the constitutional separation of church and state) or profane, though Vonnegut finds the latter charge to be a ruse to keep his opinions away from public eyes:

> My books are being thrown out of school libraries all over the country—because they're supposedly obscene. I've seen letters to small town newspapers that put *Slaughterhouse-Five* in the same class with *Deep Throat* and *Hustler* magazine. How could anybody masturbate to *Slaughterhouse-Five*?.... It's my religion the censors hate. They find me disrespectful to their idea of God Almighty. They think it's the proper business of government to protect the reputation of God. (Hayman et al. 88–89)

Slaughterhouse-Five would mark the beginning of Vonnegut's tribulations with censorship, and to the obscenity charge he would ever contend that the few four-letter words were frequently used were parts of the American vernacular. Much later in his career he would create Eugene Debs Hartke in *Hocus Pocus*, who tells his whole story with the conscious intention of avoiding profanity. The character explains his use of phrases like "when the excrement hit the air-conditioning" with his grandfather's precept: "profanity and obscenity entitle people who don't want unpleasant information to close their eyes and ears to you" (*Hocus Pocus* 4).

Clearly cataclysm has featured in Vonnegut's novels before, and many critics see his first five novels, in theme and word, getting ever closer to what he wants to say in *Slaughterhouse-Five*. (This, incidentally, is another way in which Vonnegut may be "looking back" like Lot's wife—he is drawing on characters, themes, and places from his previous fiction to build his point.) It is a storybook way of evaluating the author's career, one that Vonnegut would admonish as a theme in his later works, but to which he nevertheless concedes in interviews. Whatever he had to say on this planet, he felt he expressed in *Slaughterhouse-Five*; so successful was the book and its reaction that he felt he didn't have to work at all anymore after its publication if he didn't want to.

But Vonnegut does resist the notion that his time in Dresden was altogether life-changing and a huge preoccupation for him in his writing. Surely he wanted to tell the story; but he told *Playboy* in 1973 that "[t]he importance of Dresden in my life has been considerably exaggerated because my book about it became a best seller" (*Conversations* 94). His point is a good one. Just because *Slaughterhouse-Five* made him famous, just because it is a masterpiece, and just because it sold well commercially does not warrant undue psychoanalysis of the author, or a discounting of the themes or inspirations of his other novels.

CHAPTER FIVE

Burying Dresden

If the story of an American father's departure from his hearth is allowed to tell itself, if it is allowed to wag tongues when he isn't around, it will tell the same story it would have told a hundred years ago, of booze and wicked women.

Such a story is told in my case, I'm sure.

—Kurt Vonnegut, *Palm Sunday*

"I'M LEFT-HANDED NOW, and I'm through with novels," Vonnegut told his brother Bernard. "I'm writing a play. It's plays from now on" (*Happy Birthday, Wanda June* vii).

Even though the threat wouldn't hold up, that statement from the preface to Vonnegut's 1970 play *Happy Birthday, Wanda June* is indicative of the unbalancing he felt after completing *Slaughterhouse-Five*. During 1970, he traveled to Biafra just before the Nigerian civil war, and was also appointed to teach creative writing at Harvard University. Besides writing what he had felt for so long he needed to exorcise, Vonnegut found his family life changing too. His children, by this time, had reached adulthood. "My big house was becoming a museum of vanished childhoods— of my vanished young manhood as well (*Happy Birthday, Wanda June* vii). His twenty-five-year marriage to his high school sweetheart Jane Cox Vonnegut became unworkable and they separated in 1971. He recalls its failure in *Palm Sunday*:

> It was a good marriage for a long time—and then it wasn't. The shock of having our children no longer need us happened somewhere in there. We were both going to have to find other sorts of seemingly important work to do and other compelling reasons for working and worrying so. But I am beginning to explain, which is a violation of a rule I lay down whenever I teach a class in writing: "All you can do is tell what happened. You will get thrown out of this course if you are arrogant enough to imagine that you can tell me what happened. You do not know. You cannot know." (*Palm Sunday* 189)

But he *would* explain, saying that "it was mainly religion in a broad sense that Jane and I fought about." For Vonnegut, who had long taken pride in his rational atheism and his family's history as such, he found his wife's comfort in religion "painful." "She came to devote herself more and more to making alliances with the supernatural in her need to increase her strength and understanding—and happiness and health.... She could not understand and cannot understand why that should be painful to me, or why it should be any business of mine at all" (*Palm Sunday* 192).

He left Cape Cod and moved into a friend's apartment in New York City, where he would dedicate himself to the writing and production of a play he had written fifteen years earlier. "I was writing myself a new family and a new early manhood. I was going to fool myself, and spooks in a novel couldn't do the job," he remarked in the preface to *Happy Birthday, Wanda June* (vii). The loneliness of his Manhattan move was surely difficult for Vonnegut, who puts so much weight on the importance of a supportive family.

Wanda June ran on and off Broadway for better than six months, and was made into a film in 1971. Finding its inspiration in Homer's *Odyssey*, it satirizes the sort of Hemingway masculinity that finds honor in warfare and hunting game for sport.

Vonnegut was plagued with depression in the early seventies, and nearly suicidal. Reflecting on this time in his life he wrote:

> As for real death—it has always been a temptation to me, since my mother solved so many problems with it. The child of a suicide will naturally think of death, the big one, as a logical solution to any problem, even one in simple algebra. Question: If Farmer A can plant 300 potatoes an hour, and Farmer B can plant potatoes fifty percent faster, and Farmer C can plant potatoes one third as fast as Farmer B, and 10,000 potatoes are to be planted to an acre, how many nine-hour days will it take Farmers A, B, and C, working simultaneously, to plant 25 acres? Answer: I think I'll blow my brains out. (*Palm Sunday* 304)

His avoidance of the form of the novel continued in 1972, when people at National Education Television's WGBH in Boston approached him about a ninety-minute television show that would combine characters and stories from his novels to date. *Between Time and Timbuktu* follows Stony Stevenson (a character from *The Sirens of Titan*) through a chrono-synclastic infundibulum, where he enters various moments of *Cat's Cradle, Player Piano, God Bless You, Mr. Rosewater,* even the short story "Harrison Bergeron" and the play *Happy Birthday, Wanda June.* It aired on March 13, 1972. Later, Vonnegut would disassociate himself with the project in a letter to Vonnegut scholar Marc Leeds:

> It is what it is, and doesn't belong in the canon of my work anywhere since the idea of doing such a thing *did not in the least originate with me* (Vonnegut's emphasis.) I was so lacking in passion about what people were doing with my ideas within the demands of their own art form that I didn't even protect the title of a short story of mine, "Between Timid and Timbuktu," In small dictionaries, the word between *Timid* and *Timbuktu* is Time. (Reed and Leeds, xxiii)

During this time Vonnegut was also gaining recognition from academic circles. In 1971 he was awarded an M.A. by the University of Chicago for *Cat's Cradle,* and he was elected Vice President of P.E.N. American Center. He also became a member of the National Institute of Arts and Letters to which he would be elected Vice President in 1975. And finally he was awarded an honorary Litt.D by Hobart and William Smith College in 1974.

BREAKFAST OF CHAMPIONS

After the movie production of *Happy Birthday, Wanda June* and the television production of *Between Time and Timbuktu,* Vonnegut wrote, "I am not going to have anything more to do with film—for this reason: I don't like film" (*Between Time and Timbuktu* xiv). Citing the outrageous cost of changing something on film ("I get the heebie-jeebies every time I hear how much it will cost to fix a scene that won't work quite right"), Vonnegut prefaced *Between Time and Timbuktu* with a reversal of his previous declaration in *Happy Birthday, Wanda June:*

> I have become an enthusiast for the printed word again. I have to be that, I now understand, because I want to be a character in all of my works. I can do that in print. In a movie, somehow, the author always vanishes. Everything of mine which has been filmed so far has been one character short, and that character is me. (*Between Time and Timbuktu* xv)

But his return to print would be a complex undertaking. *Breakfast of Champions* was due out in 1971 or 1972, but Vonnegut had to call it back while he worked out its form through a writer's block, "a block most likely caused by the prospect of having to write fiction for the first time as a wildly popular figure whose words were awaited as if religious truth," (Klinkowitz, *Vonnegut in Fact* 116). The novel was originally conceived as part of *Slaughterhouse-Five,* but the two stories "just separated completely. It was like pousse-café, like oil and water—they simply were not mixable. So I was able to decant *Slaughterhouse-Five,* and what was left was *Breakfast of Champions*" (*Conversations* 108). Vonnegut put *Breakfast* on hold, shelving it several times in this period. Carol Kramer wrote for the *Chicago Tribune* in 1970: "He's offended by the amount of money he now makes. 'It's silly, not gratifying.' So he threw away his latest novel, *Breakfast of Champions*, because he didn't think it was very good and he knew it would make more money. 'I don't know what the hell I'm going to do next' (November 15, 1970). He finally did publish it for 1973.

The depression that Vonnegut suffered after completing *Slaughterhouse-Five*—facing the challenges of late middle-life and a failed marriage—had waned on *Breakfast's* completion. Vonnegut described *Breakfast of Champions* alternately as "a fiftieth birthday present to myself" (*Breakfast of Champions* 4) and as "a promise that I'm beyond [suicide] now" (*Conversations* 109). "I feel as though I am crossing the spine of a roof—" he wrote in the novel's preface, "having ascended one slope" (*Breakfast* 4).

Breakfast of Champions would be as cathartic for Vonnegut as *Slaughterhouse-Five* was, reflecting a conscious effort on Vonnegut's part to move on. "I think I am trying to clear my head of all the junk in there—the assholes, the flags, the underpants" (5), he writes. So, too, did he pledge to use many of his recurring characters for the last time. He told *Playboy*:

> At the end of Breakfast, I give the characters I've used over and over again their freedom. I tell them I won't be needing them anymore. They can pursue their own destinies. I guess that means I'm free to pursue my destiny, too. I don't have to take care of them anymore. (*Conversations* 109).

Following "two lonesome, skinny, fairly old white men on a planet which was dying fast," (*Breakfast* 7), the novel is a vicious commentary on almost everything Vonnegut perceived wrong with America in the early seventies: war (as is usually the case), notably, discrimination, and above all, commercialism and environmentalism. And the whole story is told through a patina of the possibility of insanity. William Rodney Allen, noting that Vonnegut was being medicated for depression by the writing of *Breakfast of Champions*, and that his son, Mark, had been hospitalized for a schizophrenic breakdown in 1972, comments that under these circumstances, "it is hardly surprising that [*Breakfast of Champions*] would offer the hypothesis that human beings are at the mercy of the chemical compositions of their brains" (*Vonnegut in Fact* 102).

Of the two "skinny, fairly old white men" the novel follows, our "hero," Dwayne Hoover, has his actions explained by way of body chemistry. Dwayne is losing his grip on reality already when the novel starts. He is a rich, and by all accounts a congenial Pontiac dealer whose wife had committed suicide by drinking Drano. He is a model of American economic success, a hero in the culture Vonnegut portrays, but despite the tendency for other characters in the story to measure Dwayne's life as a successful one, he remains altogether unhappy. He has sworn off love, forbidding his girlfriend, Francine Pefko, from even saying the word. Dwayne slips sufficiently to believe what he reads in a Kilgore Trout novel, where only one man in the universe has free will, and everyone else is a robot. He is violent by the novel's end, and following the lawsuits incurred during his outbursts, he is left in utter poverty.

The other line of the story follows Kilgore Trout, Vonnegut's resident washed-up science fiction writer. Trout's odyssey to the heartland of America, Midland City, begins with an invitation from another Vonnegut mainstay, Eliot Rosewater. Millionaire Rosewater has convinced the Chairman of an arts festival that Trout is perhaps the greatest living American novelist, and he is invited to speak at their new Center for the Arts. It is a surprise to Trout, who, though he had written over one hundred novels, wasn't aware that anyone had read them. Trout initially forsakes the invite as an invasion of privacy (and with a hint of agoraphobia), though he eventually decides to "leave the cage" to school the planners and patrons of the arts festival in the truth about a career in the arts. "I'm going out there to show them what nobody has ever seen at an arts festival before: a representative of all the thousands of artists who devoted their lives to a search for truth and beauty—and didn't find doodley-squat!" (*Breakfast of Champions* 37) .

Trout's journey to Midland City provides much of the disdainful commentary on the state of the culture and the planet in *Breakfast of Champions*. He is mugged in New York City, and, with only $10 to get him to Middle America, hitchhikes with a boring trucker through the "poisoned marshes of New Jersey" ruined by factories making "wash day products, cat food, [and] pop," (84) to Philadelphia, "a bomb crater, as anyone could see" (103). Trout, whom we are told is a difficult read as to whether he is being serious or not, tells the trucker that all this pollution used to worry him, too, until he realized that all this was the will of God. "I realized ... that God wasn't any conservationist, so for anyone else to be one was sacrilegious and a waste of time. You ever see one of his volcanoes or tornadoes or tidal waves?" (85).

Whether Trout is being genuine about this futility is superceded by Vonnegut's larger purpose to use Trout as an independent commentator on this America. His role is made clear early in the novel. Vonnegut calls attention to himself throughout as *auctor*, again embracing metafictional techniques that acknowledge the artificial nature of the novel. He even declares himself "on par with the Creator of the Universe" (200). In Vonnegut's game, Trout answers the question, "What is the purpose of life?":

To be
the eyes
and ears
and conscience
of the Creator of the Universe,
you fool. (57)

So as "the eyes and ears and conscience" of Vonnegut, Trout shows us much of what is wrong with America in 1972.

Things don't end well for Trout, either. Where Dwayne Hoover winds up a bum on the street, having lost everything, Trout is physically marred in Hoover's rampage. If it wasn't enough that Dwayne Hoover bites off the end of one of Trout's fingers, Vonnegut takes over at the end, hurling Trout around the world, to the sun and back, before releasing him from service. He begs for youth from his creator as Vonnegut disappears into the void.

Through both characters we obtain visions of Vonnegut's purpose, to call attention to the fact that our culture is "really a bunch of commercials, and this is intolerable" (*Conversations* 108). He explains that *Breakfast of Champions* is "a sidewalk strewn with junk, trash which I throw over my shoulders as I travel back in time to November eleventh, nineteen hundred and twenty-two" (*Breakfast of Champions* 6). That date, without coincidence Vonnegut's birthday, is also what used to be called Armistice Day, when for a magical moment at the end of the First World War, all nations who participated were silent for the 11th minute of the 11th hour of the 11th month, November, 1918. As Vonnegut works his way through the novel back to his own birthday, his purpose is "to make my head as empty as it was when I was born onto this damaged planet fifty years ago" (5). Fittingly, the last page of the novel itself is silent, consisting only of a self-portrait of Vonnegut with a tear forming from one eye.

This last page is one of dozens of drawings by Vonnegut in *Breakfast*, which are an extension of Vonnegut's use of hyperbole to make his point in his novels—the drawings along with textual descriptions assume the reader knows nothing about what is being depicted. Everything is explained in this novel. Thus in describing the Kentucky Fried Chicken franchise, we are told what a chicken is, and then treated to a drawing of a chicken, followed by a detailed examination of the process behind preparing it for consumption:

> The idea was to kill it and pull out all its feathers, and cut off its head and feet and scoop out its internal organs—and then chop it into pieces and fry the pieces, and put the pieces in a waxed paper bucket with a lid on it, so it looked like this:
> [The paragraph is followed by a crude, childish drawing of a bucket of chicken that takes up half the page.] (158)

Richard Giannone holds that since the novel is told as if the author were a survivor telling us about a lost society—like Jonah in *Cat's Cradle*—the stuff of American culture is assumed to be so foreign that it needs to be drawn. "By drawing the fruits and wares of our daily life as if they were the dinosaurs, he brings us to confront the fatal consequences of our ignominy: we are faced with, as an accomplished fact, the oblivion we are making" (Giannone 109–110). Speaking of our civilization as if it were already extinct gives Vonnegut the satiric distance he needs to critique the state of a society the same year he is writing it.

Along with the recognition he received after *Slaughterhouse-Five*, Vonnegut caught the attention of groups who saw his writing for little more than the vulgarities it contained. *Breakfast of Champions* was in part a reaction to this criticism, with its insistence on detailing the length and girth of the members of each male character, drawings of vaginas, and most famously, of his own sphincter. Most of the banning and even burning came to a head with *Slaughterhouse-Five* for its perceived anti-Christianity, but *Breakfast of Champions* was surely included among the obscene by many communities. In *Palm Sunday*, Vonnegut quotes an article in *Indianapolis Magazine* that called *Breakfast* "a riot of indecorous line drawings and misbegotten words that were suggestive of a small boy sticking out his tongue at the teacher." Vonnegut explains that the words simply reflect the way Americans really do talk, and that the drawings, among other elements, are simply jokes about our bodies. Yet he admits that such rampant use of patent vulgarity has an iconoclastic purpose as well:

> But even when I was in grammar school, I suspected that warnings about words that nice people never used were in fact lessons in how to keep our mouths shut not just about our bodies, but about many, many things—perhaps too many things. (*Palm Sunday* 220–221)

A frequent target of the censorship movement of the seventies, Vonnegut tried not to take the matter to heart, but admitted it hurt him personally. "All that is going to offend me—any writer, I think—" he said to the *New York Times* about the Supreme Court's June 1973 ruling on obscenity, "is to have the community say the writer is not a good citizen, is a poison to society instead, and this is painful to a person in any line of work, to be made to think that he is a polluter, particularly of children" (August 21, 1973).

Breakfast of Champions sold extremely well, as anyone might have predicted. His longtime following no doubt counted *Breakfast of Champions* among Vonnegut's best, though many critics were less than kind. Peter Prescott's *Newsweek* review points out some of Vonnegut's more blatant inconsistencies, such as its constant nagging that human beings are robots and machines, and then staging Rabo Karebekian's expression of awareness as "an unwavering band of light" as some kind of satisfactory resolution (Merrill 40). Prescott discards Vonnegut's hyperbole as oversimplification, and reduces his style to "smug pessimism with its coy implication that the reader is one of the author's initiates, one of the happy few" (39). These criticisms, that his young audience fails to admit that he can do wrong, that his "lobotomized English" is the result of a lack of skill more than a conscious attempt to change the way we perceive literature and the novel, would begin to eclipse the acclaim he saw after *Slaughterhouse-Five*. The publication of *Slapstick*, was fodder to this kind of criticism.

SLAPSTICK

The 1976 publication of *Slapstick* surprised many because of the speed with which it was produced. There were four years between *Rosewater* and *Slaughterhouse-Five*, and another four between the latter and *Breakfast*. But if *Slapstick* elated readers on its arrival, many were surely disappointed on its reading. Roger Sale's *New York Times* review seemed to hold Vonnegut responsible for his "slightly laid back, rather dropped out, minimally intelligent young" audience, hypothesizing that the "mistake" of Vonnegut's popularity is owing to the promise he had after writing *Cat's Cradle* and *Rosewater*, but that his novels since have become formulaic rehash. Of *Slapstick*'s refrain, "hi ho," Sale writes that "it is a gesture of contempt for all writers who are willing to be responsible for their creations; for all readers who long to read real books; for anyone whose idea of America is more complicated than Vonnegut's country of interchangeable parts full of poor people with uninteresting lives." He rails at Vonnegut for his "pithy pointlessness," saying Vonnegut "sticks with nothing long enough to imagine it, give it breathing space and air," and he accuses him of using this style as a scapegoat to avoid posing hard questions. Sale's cherry on top:

> I would be very much surprised if Tony Tanner or Robert Scholes or others who once expressed fondness for Vonnegut admire him as much now as they used to. Books that are self-confessed verbal constructions simply need more earnest and witty inventing than Vonnegut has shown himself capable of. (October 3, 1976)

Sale's truculent review prompted a letter from Scholes, among others, who defended Vonnegut, if not so much *Slapstick:*

> "Slapstick" itself seems to me a piece of whimsy, a very slight novel, and if Sale had said it isn't as good as Vonnegut's best work, I'd say "yes" to that, too. It's less ambitious, less important, less of a book than his best work. What is wrong and unfair in Sale's review is that he uses this novel to try and prove that its seven predecessors were some kind of trick, which is now exposed by the slightness of "Slapstick." (November 21, 1976)

Vonnegut was devastated. He addressed the review in his *Paris Review* interview the following year.

> *Slapstick* may be a very bad book. I am perfectly willing to believe that. Everybody else writes lousy books, so why shouldn't I? What was unusual about the reviews was that they wanted people to admit now that I had never been any good. The reviewer for the *Sunday Times* [Sale] actually asked critics who had praised me in the past to now admit in public how wrong they'd been. My publisher, Sam Lawrence, tried to comfort me by saying that authors were invariably attacked when they became fabulously well to do.... I never felt worse in my life. I felt as though I were sleeping standing up on a boxcar in Germany again. (Hayman et al. 85)

John Updike read *Slapstick* more forgivingly in the *New Yorker,* reminding readers that the level of invention within the novel— the book is easily the most science fiction work Vonnegut has penned since *The Sirens of Titan*—"looks easy only in retrospect" (Merrill 47). *Slapstick* is whimsical, Updike allows, but that should not distract us from Vonnegut's capacity to depict pain in his novels; in this regard *Slapstick* is among his best works.

Slapstick's lengthy autobiographic preface tells us squarely of the book's inspiration in the life and untimely death of Vonnegut's only sister, Alice, who died at the age of 41 of lung cancer. Comedy, obviously, has ever been intrinsic to Vonnegut's work, though he has remarked that he was always at his funniest in conjunction with his sister, and it is for her that he writes the novel. He goes further in the introduction, saying that "I had never told her so, but she was the person I had always written for" (*Slapstick* 15).

Dreamed up on an airplane to his Uncle Alex's funeral, with an empty seat between him and his only other sibling, his brother Bernard, *Slapstick* "depicts myself and my beautiful sister as monsters" (19), the twins Wilbur Daffodil-11 Swain and his sister Eliza. They are ugly, hairy, polydactyl Neanderthaloids, who become geniuses when together. A former President of the United States, Wilbur was "the final President, the tallest president, and the only one ever to be divorced while occupying the White House" (22), who, with his sister, wrote a manual on child-rearing, which ranked as the third most popular book of all time, just under the Bible and *The Joy of Cooking*.

That Wilbur and Eliza approach genius when they think together is just one of the idiosyncrasies of the world Vonnegut creates in *Slapstick*. The Chinese, for one, have figured out the same trick, and "teaching telepathically compatible specialists to think as single minds," they created super-intellects so great they eventually saw the overthrow of Western civilization. (The Chinese got the idea, incidentally, from the success of the Manhattan Project, where American and European minds came together to create the atomic bomb—yet another Vonnegutian way to hold irresponsible science accountable for cataclysm) (96). The Chinese had figured out how to miniaturize themselves, eventually to the size of microorganisms, causing a disease called the "Green Death" which wiped out most of Manhattan. Gravity became variable, like the weather, so that there may be light days and heavy days. The destruction caused by fluctuations in the earth's gravity combined with the great epidemics that swept the nation were enough to Balkanize the country, so that by the time Wilbur is in office, such figure heads as the King of Michigan have risen, and the Presidency is wholly superfluous. It's a different world in other ways, too, but the most notable is the use of government-issued, computer-generated middle names to advent loneliness in society. It is the idea with which Wilbur campaigned and won his Presidency; his slogan is the subtitle for the novel, *Lonesome No More!*

Vonnegut had seen the benefits of a huge family on his visit to Biafra, but its ultimate genesis is in his Indianapolis upbringing in a large, tight-knit family, and his ability to see how much tighter and larger it had been a few generations earlier.

Biafra made its mark on Vonnegut, who at the time experienced loneliness and familial scorn on his separation from his wife, Jane. He relates in *Biafra: A People Betrayed,*

> General Ojukwu gave us a clue, I think, as to why the Biafrans were able to endure so much so long without bitterness: They all had the emotional and spiritual strength that an enormous family can give. We asked the general to tell us about his family, and he answered that it was three thousand members strong. He knew every member of it by face, name, and reputation.
>
> A more typical Biafran family might consist of a few hundred souls. And there were no orphanages, no old people's homes, no public charities—and, early in the war, there weren't even schemes for taking care of refugees. The families took care of their own—perfectly naturally. (*Wampeters, Foma & Granfalloons* 149–150)

If his Biafra trip planted a seed for Vonnegut to write a novel professing the utility of extended families, by his 1973 *Playboy* interview it was clear that he was thinking extensively of its application in America, and he comments on the subject:

> Until recent times, you know, human beings usually had a permanent community of relatives. They had dozens of homes to

go to. So when a married couple had a fight, one or the other could go to a house three doors down and stay with a close relative until he was feeling tender again. Or if a kid got so fed up with his parents that he couldn't stand it, he could march over to his uncle's for a while. And this is no longer possible.... When Nixon is pondering what's happening to America—"Where have all the old values gone?" and all that—the answer is perfectly simple. We're lonesome. We don't have enough friends or relatives anymore. (*Conversations* 79–80)

Vonnegut blames the dissolution of the big family on industrialization and human greed. "People have to move from here to there as jobs move, as prosperity leaves one area and appears somewhere else.... You can't go home again" (*Conversations* 79). Vonnegut felt so strongly about the anthropological need to belong to a folk society and the vulnerabilities human beings face without it that he proposed the idea to the 1972 McGovern campaign:

I wanted [McGovern's running-mate] Sarge Shriver to say, "You're not happy, are you? Nobody in this country is happy but the rich people. Something is wrong. I'll tell you what's wrong: We're lonesome! We're being kept apart from our neighbors. Why? Because rich people can go on taking our money away if we don't hang together. They can go on taking our power away. They want us lonesome; they want us huddled in our houses with just our wives and kids, watching television, because they can manipulate us then. They can make us buy anything, they can make us vote any way they want. How did Americans beat the Great Depression? We banded together. In those days, members of unions called each other 'brother' and 'sister,' and they meant it. We're going to bring that spirit back. Brother and sister!.... Here's a war cry for the American people: 'Lonesome No More!'" That's the kind of demagoguery I approve of. (*Conversations* 102–103)

The government issuance of middle names to create huge artificial folk-societies as a treatment for loneliness may be an idea close to Vonnegut's heart, but it is only the latest of agents in Vonnegut's fiction that attempt to ameliorate the human condition and fail. Giannone groups Swain's plan with EPICAC XIV of *Player Piano*, which did not "computerize the nation into uniform contentment;" with Rumfoord's Church of God the Utterly Indifferent, which failed to comfort in its fatalist resignation; with Bokononism and the pseudo-paradise of San Lorenzo, which never raised living conditions for the wretched San Lorenzeans; and with Rosewater's philanthropy, which helped neither his insanity nor the lives of most recipients of his benefaction (Giannone 117).

This is yet further evidence of the author's pessimism, which is entirely expected from the spirit of novel outlined in the introduction. As Vonnegut's sister spent what were obviously her last days in a cancer ward and prepared to leave her four young children in the care of her husband, she learned from another patient that "The Brokers' Special," her husband's commuter train, had become "the only train in American railroading history to hurl itself off an open drawbridge" (12). His name was listed among the dead in that day's New York *Daily News*.

> Since Alice had never received any religious instruction, and since she had lead a blameless life, she never thought of her awful luck as being anything but accidents in a very busy place.
> Good for her.

* * *

> Exhaustion, yes, and deep money worries, too, made her say towards the end that she guessed that she wasn't really very good at life.
> Then again: Neither were Laurel and Hardy. (13)

"Slapstick" would be one of Alice's last words, and for Vonnegut, his sister's practically serene acceptance of her "awful luck" fell in the tradition of the Depression-era comedians he revered so much for providing encouragement and relief in difficult times. But in the case of Laurel and Hardy especially, the situations the two found themselves in were often so trying, and their perseverance so genuine, that they become models on how to handle the painful, lonely world Vonnegut portrays.

Vonnegut met his second wife, noted photographer and author Jill Krementz during the production of *Happy Birthday, Wanda June* in 1970, not long after he had left his family home on Cape Cod for a bachelor's apartment in New York City. He dedicates his 1974 *Wampeters, Foma, and Granfalloons* to her, saying that she helped him "regain my equilibrium" (xix). They were married November 24, 1979, the same year his next novel, *Jailbird*, arrived in bookstores.

JAILBIRD

If Vonnegut's writing peaked with *Slaughterhouse-Five* and began to wither with his seventies novels *Breakfast* and *Slapstick*, he would begin to gain ground again with *Jailbird*, which was, re- markably for an author with seven other novels in his curriculum vitae, something completely different. It is an abandon of his former settings, which usually showed some America of the distant future; *Jailbird* is stripped of his hallmark weird science in favor of a social realism wrought of actualized history. And while we have seen "historical" characters in Vonnegut before—Rumfoord based on Roosevelt, for instance—and though they certainly exist in *Jailbird*, the novel mixes seamlessly the real persons of Richard M. Nixon and Roy M. Cohn with historically inspired characters like Mary Kathleen O'Looney (based on eccentric millionaire Howard Hughes) and purely contrived characters, like our narrator and protagonist, Walter Stankiewicz.

One reason for the genre shift, as William Rodney Allen has it, may be Vonnegut's realization "after the disastrous reception of *Slapstick* that he had exhausted the possibilities of fantasy writing, he turned once again to the description of ordinary human experience" (*Understanding Kurt Vonnegut* 125). It is true that he saw success with *Mother Night*, the only other work until *Jailbird* devoid of sci-fi coloring, and that *Mother Night* was a turning point in his career. But another quality arose in *Breakfast of Champions* after he had said what he needed to say in *Slaughterhouse-Five*: the tendency to editorialize. Faced with national recognition and a secure economic future for as far as he could see, by the early seventies Vonnegut could write—and sell—almost whatever he wanted. He told *Playboy* that "as I get older, I get more didactic. I say what I really think. I don't hide ideas like Easter eggs for people to find. Now, if I have an idea, when something becomes clear to me, I don't embed it in a novel; I simply write it in an essay as clearly as I can" (*Conversations* 108). He admitted to Robert Short a few years later that "[t]here'll be more to complain about in my fiction. People will say it's not fiction anymore, it's editorializing. And, you know, the stories are getting sketchier and sketchier" (Short 300).

Thus the didacticism Vonnegut became drawn toward lent itself naturally to a more realist approach. The social criticism Vonnegut was trying to engender, for once, did not require galactic distance or hyperbolic description; the ills in *Jailbird* had already been made plain in the realities of history and the news.

In *Jailbird*, Vonnegut aims his pen at the American right-wing. His views on human dignity, the importance of communities, the living conditions of the poor, and the seeming unfairness of those born into great wealth by chance alone had always aligned him with socialist views, and Vonnegut confesses in *Jailbird's* prologue that his first vote in a national election was for Norman Thomas and Mary Hapgood on the Socialist ticket. (Thomas had taken over Socialist Party leadership after the death of Eugene Debs in 1926, namesake of Eugene Debs Hartke, the protagonist in Vonnegut's penultimate novel.)

Liberal views are commonplace in Vonnegut's fiction, and his most stalwart proliferation of socialist ideals, in *God Bless You, Mr. Rosewater,* was not so much a this-is-how-it-should-be diatribe but a ribbing to the rising Goldwater right. In much the same way, *Jailbird* does not attempt to advance a leftist policy; it assumes already that the left is correct. What it does, according to Allen, is to counter:

the prevailing American Cold War doctrine that most of the evil in the twentieth century (with the notable exception of the Nazis) was caused by left-wingers or outright communists. Recalling the repression of labor movements, the miscarriage of justice in the infamous Sacco and Vanzetti trial, and the fanatical persecution of anyone with left-wing ties in the McCarthy era, Vonnegut shows through Starbuck's account of his life that it is impossible for the right wing in America to claim the moral high ground. (*Understanding Kurt Vonnegut* 128)

Vonnegut's prologue traces the inspiration for the novel to a time just after the war when he was seeking to work for a union. He, his father, and his Harvard-educated Uncle Alex were to meet one of Alex's Harvard acquaintances, Powers Hapgood, to discuss Kurt Jr.'s interest in a career in service of a labor union. Hapgood had formerly been on the front lines of the labor movement, being jailed and even committed in his past for organizing strikes and leading pickets. He recalled over lunch that day about testifying in court:

[The judge], according to Powers Hapgood, asked him this final question just before lunch: "Mr. Hapgood," he said, "why would a man from such a distinguished family and with such a fine education choose to live as you do?"

"Why?" said Hapgood, according to Hapgood. "Because of the Sermon on the Mount, sir." (*Jailbird* xix)

Hapgood is Kenneth Whistler in *Jailbird,* who inspires Starbuck at a Harvard labor rally, and becomes his idol. Starbuck is a card-carrying Communist even while he works for the Department of Agriculture in the Roosevelt administration, but when he testifies for the House Un-American Activities Committee that his friend Leland Clewes had been a Communist, Starbuck finds himself out of a job. Nixon would remember Starbuck's services years later, and makes him his Special Advisor on Youth Affairs. His basement office becomes—through no fault of his own—a holding place for Nixon slush funds, and he serves time in federal prison for not ratting on his "associates." At the end of his sentence he coincidentally runs into his old college lover and comrade in the Party, who has married well. As Mrs Jack Graham she has become the president of the conglomerate RAMJAC, and it is her secret task to redistribute the company's wealth by creating countless vice-presidents. Like so many contrived solutions to social ills we have seen in Vonnegut's fiction before, this one does not work, either. O'Looney dies. The federal government seizes the corporation and sells off all its assets to high-bidding foreigners, using the money to pay down a tiny fraction of the national debt.

Hapgood's lunchtime defense of socialism by virtue of the Sermon on the Mount leads to a lampooning of American Christianity in *Jailbird*. Christ's Beatitudes support socialism throughout the novel, and Vonnegut derails Emil Larkin, the novel's resident born-again Christian. Defending his Evangelism to Starbuck, Larkin:

> quoted the harrowing thing that Jesus, according to Saint Matthew, had promised to say in the Person of God to sinners on Judgment Day.
>
> This is it: "Depart from me, you cursed, into the eternal fire prepared for the devil and his angels."
>
> These words appalled me then, and they appall me now. They are surely the inspiration for the notorious cruelty of Christians.
>
> "Jesus may have said that," I told Larkin, "but it is so unlike most of what else He said that I have to conclude that He was slightly crazy that day." (38)

More than Vonnegut the iconoclast here, this proselytism-as-offense is part of a series of failures on the part of American culture. The guilt-ridden, well-meaning Walter Starbuck finds nothing in the culture that lynched Sacco and Vanzetti, that allowed the RAMJAC conglomerate and the communist witch-hunts of the late 40's, that profligates hard-line Christianity to be representative of the hope of the American Dream. Vonnegut uses Christ's simple messages in the Sermon on the Mount to demonstrate the distance between this Christian nation and His teachings, which, when embraced, and offer an effective consolation in an otherwise disconsolate life.

The curious mix of fact and fiction is not a *rara avis* of 1970's fiction, but Vonnegut, uniquely, binds them by including an index to *Jailbird*. It treats such figures as Kissinger and O'Looney as equally genuine. While clearly this mix of forms is an element of *Jailbird's* postmodernism—it makes patent the fictiveness, the artificiality of the novel—Vonnegut has claimed that he had no intention of writing the book in a postmodern style. He treats the "postmodernist" label with the same ambivalence he gave to the labels "science fiction" or "black humor." The index, too, is dismissed with whimsy:

> I got the idea because I cited the Society of Indexers [in *Cat's Cradle*], whose headquarters is in England, and they wrote me and asked if I would speak to them, saying I was the only person who had ever made an indexer a character in a book.... So I asked Dell if they would please hire an indexer and find out how much it would cost to have this book indexed.... So they did, and then the juxtapositions became quite marvelous, so you know they are a very easy way to make a comic work of art. So all I did was say "Do it," and that's what came out. (Reed and Leeds, 12)

Jailbird met fair reviews, especially in relation to those of *Slapstick* and *Breakfast of Champions*. There were similar concerns by some reviewers that Vonnegut continued to shun accountability for his more challenging questions by hiding behind the postmodernist notion of the fallibility of language. Michael Wood's *New York Times* review found fault in Vonnegut's insistence on pithy sayings like "So it goes," and "And so on" once introducing a heavy topic. Wood ends:

> It is here that Vonnegut's commitment to the small change of language, to words used as jingles and charms, begins to look like a disability. Language has limits. The rest is silence, and there is more of the rest than we like to think. Vonnegut's fiction constantly alludes to this vast, silent domain. But language has

other, larger, more attractive lives. It offers a world of distinctions, it is a way of tackling experience as well as simply weathering it. It may not often result in a clarification of life, in Robert Frost's phrase, but literature provides enough of such clarifications to show us what can be done. Vonnegut's work is so likeable that its shallowness may seem to be part of its appeal. It is, however, only shallowness, a sign that the limits of language have been a little too warmly welcomed. (September 9, 1979)

But Vonnegut appeared to gain a second wind with *Jailbird*. Of its creation, he told Charles Reilly in a 1980 interview that "I found myself thinking that I had written two books over the last few years that I hadn't liked very much. The critics seemed similarly displeased with them. I hadn't liked much of what I had written in this decade, in fact, and I began to wonder if I was ever going to write another good book, because I had liked a lot of the older ones. But I certainly like this one." (*Conversations* 220–221).

Vonnegut followed *Jailbird* with the text to *Sun Moon Star*, a children's book in conjunction with illustrator Ivan Chermayeff about the birth of Christ. Then, in 1981, he released *Palm Sunday*, a follow-up of sorts to 1975's *Wampeters, Foma, & Granfalloons*, containing less available essays, interviews, and speeches in addition to original autobiographical material. It has proved to be an invaluable source for information on Vonnegut's life, and, stylized with his own commentary, offers uncanny insight to the man and his opinions. He would follow that ten years later with *Fates Worse Than Death*. At the age of sixty, thirty years after the publication of *Player Piano*, he published his tenth novel, *Deadeye Dick*, in 1982.

CHAPTER SIX

Ten Years More

But suppose we foolishly got rid of our nuclear weapons, our Kool-Aid, and an enemy came over here and crucified us....

If we were up on crosses, with nails through our feet and hands, wouldn't we wish that we still had hydrogen bombs, so that life could be ended everywhere? Absolutely.

We know of one person who was crucified in olden times, who was supposedly as capable as we or the Russians are of ending life everywhere. But He chose to endure agony instead. All he said was, "Forgive them, Father—they know not what they do."

—Kurt Vonnegut, *Fates Worse Than Death*

VONNEGUT SCHOLAR PETER J. REED interviewed the writer in the autumn of 1982, following the release of his latest novel, *Deadeye Dick*:

Reed: I've spoken about the artificiality of breaking up your work into segments or periods, but I wanted to ask about the shape of fiction overall.... It is common to see the works, the novels, as breaking up into six and four, or for people to talk about the works up through *Slaughterhouse-Five* and what's come since. Do you have any fear of that yourself?

Vonnegut: No, that's legitimate. All that annoys me about arbitrariness is that history is divided up into decades, you know, so I am a sixties person. Just what the hell was I doing in the seventies and eighties?.... But in terms of my personal life, you're absolutely right: I had a sense of completion, of the mission accomplished with *Slaughterhouse-Five*, and after that I had to start a new business, a major new business, that was all. That was closed out, and that was satisfying to me, and that was all I ever expected to do with my life. (Reed and Leeds 3)

The three novels Vonnegut wrote in the eighties, *Deadeye Dick* (1982), *Galápagos* (1985), and *Bluebeard* (1987), would comprise his most productive period ever, and, while each is highly individualized, they represent a renaissance for the writer that began with in 1979 with *Jailbird*. *Deadeye Dick* is dedicated to his second wife, Jill Krementz, who no doubt did much to spur this new era of creativity. They adopted a daughter, Lily, in 1982, the same year of *Deadeye Dick's* publication.

Despite what critics had to say about his last few novels, Vonnegut's speaking engagements continued to be in high demand in throughout the eighties. Jerome Klinkowitz's unmatched examination of Vonnegut as a public figure notes that "like F. Scott Fitzgerald in the 1930's, the conservative 1980's were less fond of Vonnegut's sometimes revolutionary attitudes from an era which had seemed to run its course." Even so, his lecture, "How to Get a Job Like Mine," would have audiences at capacity, "applauding whichever work-in-progress he would conclude with" (Klinkowitz, *Vonnegut in Fact* 21).

DEADEYE DICK

Deadeye Dick would continue Vonnegut's movement from fantastic or alter-American settings, and, like *Jailbird,* presents a socially real picture of a guilt-ridden narrator relating the solecisms of his past. And where *Jailbird* confined Vonnegut's voice to the introductory material, *Deadeye Dick* does likewise. Vonnegut tells us openly, however, how to read the novel for autobiographical clues:

> I will explain the main symbols of this book.
> There is an unappreciated, empty arts center in the shape of a sphere. This is my head as my sixtieth birthday beckons me.
> There is a neutron bomb explosion in a populated area.
> This is the disappearance of so many people I cared about in Indianapolis when I was starting out to be a writer. Indianapolis in there, but the people are gone.
> Haiti is New York City, where I live now.
> The neutered pharmacist who tells the tale is my declining sexuality. The crime he committed in childhood is all the bad things I have done. (*Deadeye Dick* xii–xiii)

Certainly the crime the narrator, Rudy Waltz, committed has origins in Vonnegut's own life. Rudy's father, like Kurt Vonnegut, Sr., was a collector of firearms. The young Rudy accidentally shoots and kills a pregnant woman with a gun from his father's extensive (and unguarded) collection. "You know, I did that," Vonnegut told interviewer Zoltan Abadi-Nagy in 1989, "I didn't kill anybody. But I fired a rifle, out over Indianapolis. I didn't hit anybody as far as I know." He goes on to say that the experience frightened him into his adult years. And just as Vonnegut explains that he fired the gun because "it was just very easy to fire" (Reed and Leeds, 21–22), so the young Rudy Waltz just squeezes the trigger, loosing a bullet over Midland City (*Deadeye Dick* 62).

Some critics have assigned a deeper source for Rudy's guilt. *Palm Sunday* contains Vonnegut's essay "Embarrassment," in which he describes "a bad dream I have dreamed for as long as I can remember.... In that dream, I know that I have murdered an old woman a long time ago. I have lead an exemplary life ever since" (*Palm Sunday* 189). Vonnegut wonders in the essay whether the woman may be his mother. William Rodney Allen psychoanalyzes: "It seems reasonable to conclude that Vonnegut's dream about killing an older person may reflect anger at both his parents and that his sense of shame in part proceeds from that source" (*Understanding Kurt Vonnegut* 140). Rudy's parents do in fact resemble Vonnegut's own: Otto Waltz is a would-be artist, and his fascination with firearms, it is suggested, has roots in offsetting a not-so-masculine trade; Rudy's mother, like Vonnegut's, was born rich, took a change in financial status poorly, and failed as a mother. *Deadeye Dick*, then, when read autobiographically, may be, as Allen has it, "Vonnegut's most intensely personal fictional exploration of his unhappy relationship with his parents" (139).

Deadeye Dick may also be Vonnegut's self-inflicted penance for the failure of *Happy Birthday, Wanda June*. Rudy's one chance at renewal, his play *Katmandu*, is as unready as Vonnegut's was, and though *Wanda* ran for some time on and off Broadway, *Katmandu* follows in its failure to advance its philosophy. On the one hand, Vonnegut's novels are always filled with depressed, sometimes failed artists, and a terrible play is an acceptable vehicle for that. When asked about this recurring character Vonnegut cites the University of Iowa study done when he taught at the Writer's Workshop in 1965, which found all the writers "strikingly depressed" (*Conversations* 281). On the other hand, writing about *Katmandu* may be cathartic for Vonnegut in the same way *Breakfast of Champions* had been; he told *Playboy* that writing was therapeutic, and felt that "*Breakfast* will be the last of the therapeutic books" (*Conversations* 109). Setting his failed play from ten years back into fiction, however, may have been a way to treat that part of his past. In fact, *Breakfast of Champions* and *Deadeye Dick* have other similarities as well. Besides sharing the same setting, Midland City, with its Sugar Creek and its arts center, many of the same characters return, and we even discover why Dwayne Hoover's wife committed suicide. Perhaps *Deadeye Dick* is a penance of sorts for *Breakfast of Champions*, too.

The novel is ostensibly Vonnegut sounding off on gun control, with Otto Waltz saying "most of the things the National Rifle Association still says about how natural and beautiful it is for Americans to have love affairs with guns," just before his twelve-year-old son Rudy nonsensically fires a shot over the city that hits the pregnant Eloise Metzger "right between the eyes" (*Deadeye Dick* 66). The police chief accidentally blows August Gunther's head off with a ten-gauge shotgun, and the crime is covered up with the help of Otto Waltz. George Metzger's letter to the newspaper a day and a half after his wife was shot is a plea putting the culpability of his wife's death on the gun (87). Moreover, Vonnegut's statement on the danger inherent in firearms is a microcosm of the national irresponsibility about weapons development. Vonnegut has the inhabitants of Midland City and its surrounding areas exterminated by the accidental deployment of a neutron bomb.

There is social commentary in the nature of the destruction here, too, because though the bomb kills about one hundred thousand people, it leaves all the property intact, granting "about ten days or so" of news coverage (33). Rudy questions the nature of the loss: "Since all the property is undamaged, has the world lost anything it loved?" (34). It is a grand extension of the same questions posed by Paul Proteus and Eliot Rosewater: is there love in the world for people who are economically useless? Since it is everywhere shown that money and materialism are precisely what is useless and even perilous, Vonnegut's one conclusion throughout his novels is the value of human decency. Eliot Rosewater says, "Godamnit, you've got to be kind." Malachi Constant says the purpose of life is "to love whoever is around to be loved." Vonnegut's own son Mark, in his memoir about his battle with manic depression (originally thought to be schizophrenia), *Eden Express*, says "We are here to help each other get through this thing, whatever it is." Courtesy and decency in the human community is the only defense against the absurd catastrophes of the universe.

Another Vonnegutian theme that returns in *Deadeye Dick* is the tendency for people to create fictions, stories for themselves. When it becomes clear that Rudy fired the shot that killed Mrs. Metzger, his father immediately and dramatically takes the blame for the crime. Rudy's older brother Felix says later that their father confessed because "[i]t was the first truly consequential adventure life had ever offered him" (69). Otto Waltz accepts the blame and jail sentence because it would make a good story. Rudy's coping mechanism for all his worst memories, such as his confrontation with George Metzger, husband of slain Eloise, is to turn them into plays. It is a way to circumvent reality. "The characters are actors. Their speeches and movements are stylized, arch" (83–84).

Vonnegut resists stepping into the action of the story (and in all his other later novels from *Jailbird* on, with the exception of his farewell, *Timequake*), but he does allow himself a cameo. In one of the novel's metafictional highlights, Rudy finds himself smiling at Celia's funeral. When he becomes aware of this, he looks around to see if anyone has noticed.

> One person had. He was at the other end of our pew, and he did not look away when I caught him gazing at me. He went right on gazing, and it was I who faced forward again. I had not recognized him. He was wearing large sunglasses with mirrored lenses. He could have been anyone. (198)

The allusion is to Kurt Vonnegut of *Breakfast of Champions*, where the author is described as wearing the same mirrored lenses. Kilgore Trout, we know, sees mirrors as leaks—holes into another universe. Here, then, Vonnegut places his avatar in the text as a link to his other fictional universes.

By this time in reviews it is acknowledged that Vonnegut has a fan base (most reviewers cannot resist throwing in the word "young") that will remain uncritical of his work so long as it contains enough of his old mainstays. The *New York Times* printed a mediocre review by Christopher Lehmann-Haupt that spent most of its column space being thankful that the novel did not contain a repeating tagline like "so it goes." Conversely, Loree Rackstraw, albeit a former student of Vonnegut's at Iowa, wrote that it "will likely stand as Vonnegut's most tightly crafted and complex work to date" (Merrill 54). Her review, in fact, says much to support that statement. She has Vonnegut's overarching concern succinctly: "life is often a cruel accident; the dilemma of humanity is how to stay alive with decency in the face of that reality" (54).

It wouldn't be until 1991's *Fates Worse Than Death* that Vonnegut would discuss publicly his 1984 suicide attempt, and even then, thinly. "I went briefly apeshit in the 1980's in an effort to get out of life entirely, and wound up playing Eightball in a locked ward for thirty days instead" (*Fates Worse Than Death* 93). "I was pissed off," he told the *Washington Post,* but declined to elaborate on one specific cause. "If I do myself in sometime, and I might, it will be because of my mother's example. If I really get pissed off, screw it all." David Streitfeld, the author of the article, wrote that "[i]t's not a coincidence that his suicide attempt came in 1984, at a moment when liberalism was on the run and, worse luck, hardly anybody minded" (Streitfeld c.01). Whether or not it was Ronald Reagan that drove Vonnegut to suicide, he was certainly no friend to that administration. But by the early 90's he seemed resigned to continue living. "[Suicide is] on my mind all the time. But I tried as hard as I could to kill myself, without any luck. So my feeling is, the hell with it." Given these comments, it is rather extraordinary that he would write three more novels and the non-fiction *Fates* between his attempted suicide and this interview.

GALÁPAGOS

Chance is yet again given a major role in Vonnegut's next novel, which spans a million years in duration. Unlike the social realities of *Jailbird* and *Deadeye Dick* with their guilty, Howard Campbell-like narrators reflecting inwardly on a dubious life, *Galápagos* externalizes catastrophe in the tradition of *Slapstick* and *The Sirens of Titan,* though in this surely fantastic tale, science trumps science fiction. We again have the decimation of the human species, but like everything else in *Galápagos,* it is done slowly, over time, by means of a tiny virus affecting the human ovum, making reproduction impossible for everyone save a group of ten people collected on Santa Rosalia, a contrived island in the *Galápagos.* The descendants of that bottlenecked gene pool, thanks to circumstantial mutation and natural adaptation, become seal-like fish-eaters living in bliss, having lost the big brains that Vonnegut sees as the cause of so much mischief.

Vonnegut has always been interested in Darwin and nature, and the book has its genesis in a trip Vonnegut and his wife made to the Galapagos islands in 1981. "Of course, I was fascinated by the island's natural life," he told the *New York Times*. "We had advantages Darwin didn't have. Our guides all had graduate degrees in biology. We had motorboats to move us around the islands more easily then rowboats could when Darwin visited the *Galápagos* in the 1830's. And, most important, we knew Darwin's theory of evolution, and Darwin didn't when he was there" (October 6, 1985).

Adherence to Darwin's theory—and to the science of the story in general—was of great concern to Vonnegut in writing *Galápagos*. He rejects utterly the notion of the "survival of the fittest," unsurprisingly, and Vonnegut goes to great lengths in the novel to show that chance plays more in determining the circumstances of life than strength. The "Nature Cruise of the Century" that carries ten humans alone away from the diseased mainland had been originally intended for what many in American culture would consider to be great examples of human beings: celebrities. As luck would have it, though, the ten people that do make it to Santa Rosalia have the genetic configurations to allow humans to survive on the rocky islands of the *Galápagos*, including a fur covered girl whose mother was subjected to radiation after the atomic bomb was dropped on Hiroshima. Vonnegut had read the writings of Harvard biologist Stephen J. Gould in preparation for the book, and he was delighted to receive a letter from Gould after *Galápagos* was published, affirming that its science is plausible. "He thought it was a wonderful roman a clef about evolutionary theory and also proves how random the selection is. He said that the fur-covered baby was a good mutation, that it was a common one. So it's reputable scientifically; I was as worried as much about that one as anything" (*Conversations* 252)

Vonnegut was tortured by the novel's demand for scientific plausibility as much as the technical problems of telling a tale that spans a million years. "As an atheist, I couldn't have God watch" (*Conversations* 251), he said of the viewpoint character. No doubt pleasing to Vonnegut's longtime readers, the narrator's identity is hinted at sufficiently that we may guess (before it is made clear) that the story is being told by the ghost of Leon Trotsky Trout, son of Vonnegut's wretched alter-ego Kilgore Trout, who speaks to us from the year 1001986 A.D. as a ghost writing the story "with air on air" (*Galápagos* 290). The author is double served: a million years gives him the distance he needs to comment on society (predominantly the Vietnam War in *Galápagos*, though the usual suspects do show up), and it extends the theme of evolution, since the narrator is the transformed offspring of a former Vonnegut mouthpiece.

The genius of *Galápagos* lies most especially in the way it is structured. The novel is split in two parts. "The Thing Was" is the story of the circumstances under which these ten alone came to the island of Santa Rosalia. "And the Thing Became" shows how the spawn of less than a dozen humans evolved to forsake intelligence for animal happiness, a condition lacking the range of human emotion. The first, larger half of the book is deliberately convoluted, with a confusing mix of personalities and circumstances meant to reflect the dazzling complexity of the human condition. Ever a dabbler in experimental fiction, Vonnegut writes the second half with the express purpose of mirroring the de-evolution that takes place over the novel's million years, and in that, "The Thing Became" is weaker and less sophisticated than "The Thing Was." Vonnegut has never owned up to subscribing to European post-structuralist philosophies, but William Rodney Allen shows how *Galápagos* embraces the precepts of deconstruction. "Vonnegut uses the language of the novel to undermine its own ground, suggesting that the complexities of human, self consciousness have meaning only in relation to each other, and little or no relation to events outside themselves. *Galápagos* uses intelligence to undercut intelligence, language to undercut language" (*Understanding Kurt Vonnegut* 158).

Even the Vonnegutian hallmarks have evolved in *Galápagos*. First, readers will notice the absence of a Vonnegut mainstay since *Slaughterhouse-Five*—the author's introduction. His familiar taglines, too, which never really recovered in the eyes of critics since Roger Sale's review of *Slapstick*, have practically vanished. Of course, Vonnegut cannot resist innovation. Idiosyncrasies like asterisks next to the names of people who have died, and quotations throughout the text from a computer called Mandarax (a clear symbol of human knowledge with allusions to the apple that felled Adam and Eve) which provides much of the humor in its unexpected "commentaries."

Galápagos resists the utter pessimism inherent in his other works, and this is the most startling evolution. It is evident as early as the epigraph, Anne Frank's famous quote, "In spite of everything, I still believe people are really good at heart." Trout confirms that the loss of intelligence, for all the troubles caused by our big brains, is not a desirable event after watching what humans have become after a million years.

> Nothing ever happens around here that I haven't seen or heard many times before. Nobody, surely, is going to write Beethoven's Ninth Symphony—or tell a lie, or start a Third World War.
>
> Mother was right: Even in the darkest times, there really was still hope for humankind. (*Galápagos* 259)

BLUEBEARD

After his list of 15 other works at the beginning of *Bluebeard,* Vonnegut writes, "Enough! Enough!" He is 65 in 1987, and though it has only been two years since the issue of *Galápagos,* Vonnegut insists that he is tired, and that he cannot write as fast as he used to.

Bluebeard resurrects Rabo Karebekian, the minimalist painter introduced first in *Breakfast of Champions,* whose painting of an unwavering band of light representing animal awareness provided Vonnegut with the reason we are all *not* machines. *Bluebeard* is presented as Karebekian's autobiography, and it tells as much about his life as it does "this past troubled summer" (*Bluebeard* 1). Rabo is shown to be a broken, weak man, and his confrontations with newcomer Circe Berman provide much of the dramatic tension in the novel. Circe is a prying, rather strong willed woman who writes books about adolescent problems. She concludes that Karebekian's discontent is largely due to his poor relations with women.

Bluebeard, of course, gives Vonnegut the opportunity to opine on any number of social issues, but it is the relationship between art and war, and his fascination with the sexual revolution that really drive the plot. The title refers to the folktale of *Bluebeard*, which Vonnegut sets down, "for the sake of the young readers":

> Bluebeard is a fictitious character in a very old children's tale, possibly based loosely on a murderous nobleman of long ago. In the story, he has married many times. He marries for the umpteenth time, and brings his latest child bride back to his castle. He tells her that she can go into any room but one, whose door he shows her.
>
> Bluebeard is either a poor psychologist or a great one, since all the new wife can think about is what might be behind the door. So she takes a look when she thinks he isn't home, but he really is home.
>
> He catches her just at the point she is gazing aghast at the bodies of all his former wives in there, all of whom he has murdered, save for the first one, for looking behind the door. The first one got murdered for something else. (46)

Karebekian has a secret room, too—the locked, windowless potato barn is a source of intrigue for Berman. Inside is a vast painting of photographic quality featuring a terrible scene after war, with over five thousand figures portrayed in precise detail—the largest as big as a cigarette, and the smallest requiring a magnifying glass. Refugees wander across the countryside; former POW's chase down their former guards; soldiers from every imaginable army swarm the valley. When Circe says that there don't seem to be any women, he tells her that half of the people who have just left the concentration camps and the insane asylums are women, they just don't look the part; all the healthy women are hiding in root cellars at the very edges of the huge canvas, "putting off being raped as long as possible" (286). The painting is called, "Now It's the Women's Turn."

It is his most vocal position on the women's movement yet. At first, "Now It's the Women's Turn" appears to signify just another hazard of humanity's propensity towards war. But the depiction of the young women hiding in roots cellars is just one evocative example of the mistreatment of women in *Bluebeard,* who so often—as in the titular folktale—find their own doom a door away. Karebekian recalls the murder of women in the Armenian genocide the Turks conducted on his parent's generation; his employer Dan Gregory abuses his lover Marilee Kemp, who, also beaten by her father in youth and raped by the football team in high school, provides much of the feminist commentary in the novel. When Rabo hints to her about his numerous sexual encounters during the war, Marilee translates, "wherever you went there were women who would do anything for food or protection for themselves and the children and the old people, since the young men were dead or gone away." She goes on to contend that "the whole point of war is to put women in that condition. It's always men against women, with the men only pretending to fight among themselves" (224). Her story of her cook, Lucrezia, elaborates the sacrifices women have made during the conflict, and assigns blame:

> "Do you have an artificial leg?" she said.
>
> "No," I said.
>
> "Lucrezia, the woman who let you in, lost a leg along with an eye. I thought maybe you'd lost one, too."
>
> "No such luck," I said.
>
> "Well—" she said, "early one morning she crossed a meadow, carrying two precious eggs to a neighbor who had given birth to a baby the night before. She stepped on a mine. We don't know what army was responsible. We do know the sex. Only a male would design and bury a device that ingenious. Before you leave, maybe you can persuade Lucrezia to show you all the medals she won."
>
> And then she added: "Women are so useless and unimaginative, aren't they? All they ever think of planting in the dirt is the seed of something beautiful or edible. The only missile they can ever think of throwing at anybody is a ball or a bridal bouquet." (224–225)

Commentary like this provides the double meaning for

Karebekian's realist masterpiece hidden in the potato barn. Under these circumstances, "Now It's the Women's Turn" not only provides a vivid description of the horrors of war, but suggests moreover that perhaps the time has come for the world to allow women to be the global decision-makers. Vonnegut told interviewers Allen and Smith in 1987 that in the wake of constant weapons development and increasing armament, "now it's the women's turn—it had better be" (*Conversations* 271).

Along with further invectives against war and a strong advocacy of feminism, *Bluebeard* is about art. Vonnegut says in *Fates Worse Than Death* that he got the idea for the book after writing an article for *Esquire* about Jackson Pollock, who, spearheading the Abstract Expressionist movement of the post-World War II period, "made himself a champion and connoisseur of the appealing accidents which more formal artists worked hard to exclude from their performances" (*Fates* 42). *Bluebeard* posits that Pollock and other Abstract Expressionists (Karebekian among them) *had* to turn to accidents to inspire beauty in others following the maelstrom of the war. Vonnegut speaks to this connection between abstract art and the horrors of World War II in the *Esquire* article, reprinted in *Fates*:

> Has any theory of artistic inspiration ever urged painters so vehemently, while they worked, to ignore life itself—to ignore life utterly? in all the Abstract Expressionist paintings in museums and on the walls of art lovers, and in the vaults of speculators, there is very little to suggest a hand or a face, say, or a table or a bowl of oranges, or a sun or a moon—or a glass of wine.
>
> And could any moralist have called for a more appropriate reaction by painters to World War II, to the death camps and Hiroshima and all the rest of it, than pictures without persons or artifacts, without even allusions to the blessings of Nature? A full moon, after all, had come to be known as a "bomber's moon." Even an orange could suggest a diseased planet, a disgraced humanity, if someone remembered, as many did, that the commandant of Auschwitz and his wife and children, under the greasy smoke from the ovens, had had good food every day. (44)

For all this praise of abstract painting, though, much of *Bluebeard* deals with the advantages of representational and non-representational art. Prying houseguest Berman favors the former, and her challenge to Karebekian's artistic career results in the illustrative autobiography he pens. As the similarities between Karebekian's life and experimental style of art develop with Vonnegut's, Karebekian, in turn, defends Vonnegut's career. Both, of course, have embraced new forms of art following their experiences with the atrocities of the Second World War.

Vonnegut is consistent in his usual preoccupations. Karebekian is a guilty man like Starbuck and Campbell and Waltz, among others. Suicides are ubiquitous. Karebekian refers often to the times with his surrogate families, his band of artist-warriors in the camouflage detail in the war, and the artists who founded the new movement in New York City. He is lonely in his old age. The horrors of warfare are examined here in perhaps the most detail since *Slaughterhouse-Five*. There are even double-agents in the characters of Marilee and her homosexual husband (who, not accidentally, treats her better than any of her former, masculine significants), and though the role does not serve as a glimpse of a different reality like Proteus' double-dealing in *Player Piano,* the proposition does allow her to evaluate democracy versus fascism. (This in fact may be a vehicle to illustrate the ways in which women are something less than participants in American politics; it is not until she has married to the rank of Contessa that it becomes imperative for her to make a decision on the form of government that is best.)

There are innovations of note. Like its predecessor *Galápagos,* *Bluebeard* ends rather happily. The presence of a full and lively household, like the tight-knit fisher-people that humans have become in *Galápagos,* fulfills Vonnegut's fantasy of the large, supportive family. Vonnegut's introduction is minuscule when viewed against some of his former works, and serves mostly to advance his own view that too much money has been spent on "human playfulness," which includes not only works of art, but those other causes of celebrity—professional sports, music, etc. Of this pithy author's note Klinkowitz writes, "it is to be emphasized that with this work Vonnegut no longer stands in front to suggest what his novel is but rather wishes to clarify what it is not" (*Vonnegut in Fact* 128). His old hallmarks like childish hyperbole, and meaningful, repetitive taglines are ghosted, too, though they have not seen center stage since *Slapstick*.

Even Later Works

> *To the Editor:*
> *A woman I had dinner with the other night said to me that the atmosphere in this country since the Persian Gulf war is like that at a party in a beautiful home, with everybody being polite and bubbly. And there is this stink coming from somewhere, getting worse all the time, and nobody wants to be the first to mention it.*
>
> —Kurt Vonnegut, Letter to the *New York Times,*
> March 27, 1991

HOCUS POCUS

Vonnegut stayed on his college lecture circuit through the eighties, speaking usually to capacity crowds. But by 1988 he had stopped altogether, citing the apathy of his audiences to the issues he had been addressing for his career. He blamed his old nemesis television in a 1990 interview for the *Chicago Tribune:*

> I think TV has distanced people from everything that's going on. TV requires no response from the audience whatsoever. They like

it or they don't like it, but it's just another show they watched last night.

There are perfectly awful messages around and there I was volunteering to deliver them. What I said in my lectures was that had my German family remained in Germany instead of coming over here, how would we have reacted to the rise of Hitler? My guess was that we wouldn't have done much about it until it was too late.

But we face a threat now, and it's terrible. It's not as personalized as Hitler was, but what we're doing to the biosphere is going to be as dire as Auschwitz—without IG Farben having to make poison gas. I felt I should start yelling about that in public the way I should have been, had I been in Germany in the 1920's, yelling about Hitler coming to power. (September 2, 1990)

Vonnegut's disappointment with the 1980's is expressed in *Hocus Pocus* (1990), perhaps his most pessimistic book to date. It is classic Vonnegut. Two months shy of 68 at the publication of his thirteenth novel, *Hocus Pocus* does just about everything Vonnegut has been successful with over his forty-year career.

The novel is composed of the scribblings of Eugene Debs Hartke, Lieutenant Colonel in the United States Army and last American to be airlifted from the roof of the American Embassy in Saigon, marking the U.S.'s embarrassing withdrawal from Vietnam. Hartke writes from the future, the year 2001, in an America Vonnegut perceived as the logical extension of behavior he witnessed in the Reagan years. The country is bankrupt, having sold most of itself to foreign interests. Du Pont is a subsidiary of Germany's IG Farben; the *New York Times* is published by Koreans; Anheuser-Busch is owned by Italians; and the Japanese treat their vast percentage of America much the same way America treated Vietnam: they are an Army occupying a nation. Japanese holdings of note include Blue Cross/Blue Shield, hospitals, and prisons, which have been privatized and run for profit. One such venture is the New York State Maximum Security Adult Correctional Institution at Athena, across the lake from Hartke's post at Tarkington College, a small school for the dim children of the upper class. The Foucauldian relationship between these neighboring institutions is drawn early and made clear when Hartke loses his teaching job at Tarkington for sexual misconduct and poor patriotism, and relocates across the lake to the all-Black and Hispanic prison. Racism has exploded to such a degree by 2001 that when the inmates pull off a jailbreak and make across the frozen lake and lay siege to Tarkington (an event at least partly ameliorated by the lessened student population on break), Hartke is accused of being the mastermind, since it is thought that the inmates couldn't possibly have pulled it off on their own. He is jailed in the same prison.

Hocus Pocus is Vonnegut's continued disillusion with American culture. This should not surprise readers of even one single other Vonnegut text, but in *Hocus Pocus* he appears to be exacerbated to the degree that the humor, where present, is at its darkest.

Vonnegut keeps himself out of the book. As in *Mother Night* the book greets us not with a personal note from the author but from a pretended "Editor's Note," in which he has avowed to allow the narrator Hartke to tell his own story. The absence of autobiographical material places the onus of sociological comment on Vietnam veteran Hartke, "whose concerns with national policy," according to Vonnegut scholar Jerome Klinkowitz, "make it Vonnegut's most committed fictive work of social and political argument" (*Vonnegut in Fact* 132).

Hartke's dystopia is shadowed by his experiences as a commander in Vietnam. As he recalls his youth, he spends great effort tracing the line of circumstances under which he forewent his acceptance to the University of Michigan and a degree in journalism for certain grooming as an officer at West Point. He interjects his thoughts on his life in Vietnam sporadically in his narration, effecting the reader to understand the gravity of what he experienced there. Because at the time he writes he is a changed man—or at least a changing man—his insights on American action in Vietnam have a special authenticity.

Hartke spent his last year in Vietnam working in public information, spinning tales of American blunders to the press. We have seen Vonnegut's attitudes towards public relations people before; his own experiences in that trade at General Electric have supplied many of his harsher words against those who would compromise truth—and, ultimately, democracy—for self-interest or, in the case of American involvement in Vietnam, to save face. But Hartke's old post in information doesn't just expose government doublespeak: he is in effect a double-agent, that tried and true Vonnegut archetype, since he is on the *other side* now. It is Vonnegut's intention and expectation that this other side is *our side.*

It is the narrator's position as a disillusioned commander, an erstwhile insider addressing the rest of the world, a one-time public relations man who has decided to write the truth, who makes this kind of information available to Vonnegut. Klinkowitz observes that the author must keep his autobiography out of *Hocus Pocus* in order to comment on an era that does not belong to him. Vonnegut's criticisms must be voiced through the fictitious Hartke because:

> beginning with the Vietnam War and following through the internationalization of American business and industry during the 1990s, they are not exclusively of Kurt Vonnegut's self or generation. For once, his autobiography is not at issue; rather, just as a general knowledge of Darwinian science carries the reader into *Galapagos* and even a rudimentary knowledge of American art history does the same in *Bluebeard*, a character speaking for a span of history Kurt Vonnegut has himself addressed as a spokesperson must bear the fictive burden. (*Vonnegut in Fact* 132)

To put it another way, Vonnegut must give up on blatant autobiographical comment because his points here are better made by someone closer to the action, even if that person is a fiction.

So through Hartke we learn how the stoned, drunk, and hapless soldiers of Vietnam were responsible for "several of the most gruesome accidents I had to explain," all of which were ascribed to "human error" (*Hocus Pocus* 28). He tells the story of a 15-year-old Viet Cong sniper caught and mutilated by American troops. Hartke makes it clear that he would never condone such actions under his command, relating how he even stopped the less-visceral habit of one of his platoons who were leaving aces of spades on the bodies of enemies. He notes then:

> What a footsoldier can do to a body with his pip-squeak technology is nothing, of course, when compared with the ordinary, unavoidable, perfectly routine effects of aerial bombing and artillery. One time I saw the severed head of a bearded old man resting on the guts of an eviscerated water buffalo, covered with flies in a bomb crater by a paddy in Cambodia. The plane whose bomb made the crater was so high that it couldn't even be seen from the ground. But what the bomb did, I would have to say, sure beat the ace of spades for a calling card. (46)

As much as Vietnam is an embarrassment and preoccupation for Hartke and Vonnegut, it is only one of the broader issues the author would like to expose as American foppery from the last fifty years. Central is the notion that the very rich, the American ruling class, have betrayed what little responsibility they once had to the country and have "taken the money and run," as it were. "You once had people like Andrew Carnegie and Henry Ford who were just nuts about manufacturing," Vonnegut told the *Chicago Tribune.* "You couldn't get them away from the damn factory, the noise and glamour of it. And all that's died down." In his view, these less-motivated captains of industry, the descendants of those who built their fortunes, are too lazy or stupid (like the student body of Tarkington College), or in any case too far removed to control the family fortune:

> You know, all the Rockefeller heirs—I know several of them and they're nice enough people—but they want the capital. They don't want the responsibility for this broad spectrum of businesses that the Rockefeller fortune is invested in. They don't know anything about manufacturing. They don't know anything about chemistry. They don't know anything about math. They don't know anything about labor relations and they don't want to. They just want to sell it and get the $17 million or $3 million or whatever and redecorate the house. (September 2, 1990)

The process that began with the automation of factories, which, of course, replaced humans with machines, thereby requiring less management eventuates in "the selling off of everything in favor of one last generation's self-privilege" (*Vonnegut in Fact* 132). America in *Hocus Pocus* is in shambles, and the withdrawal of vast sums from circulation, and worse yet, the apathy of the new proprietors is not helping. When the prison break occurs at Athena, the Japanese guards run and hide in the surrounding forest. "This wasn't their country, and guarding prisons wasn't a sacred mission or anything like that. It was just a business" (*Hocus Pocus* 85).

Vietnam and the increasing foreign proprietorship of America are only two of the biggest headlines of bad news. Racism has effectively segregated society once again, and the final burst of the overpopulated correctional facility at Athena (which has seen exponential growth while Tarkington's enrollment remained at a static three hundred) is, as *The Nation* puts it, "right out of Uncle Tom's Cabin" (Leonard 424). Television is held accountable for its muddling of reality in the American mind:

> I told Donner the Warden wanted to see him, but he didn't seem to know who I was. I felt as though I were trying to wake up a mean drunk. I used to have to do that a lot in Vietnam. A couple of times the mean drunks were Generals. The worst was a visiting Congressman.
>
> I thought I might have to fight Donner before he realized that *Howdy Doody* wasn't the main thing going on. (*Hocus Pocus* 232)

And:

> Life was like an ocean liner to a lot of people who weren't in prison, too, of course. And their TV sets were portholes through which they could look while doing nothing, to see all the World was doing with no help from them.
>
> Look at it go! (230)

So many of these modern ills are symptomatic of "the complicated futility of ignorance," the label Hartke tags the

numerous attempts of the uneducated Tarkington College's founder to create a perpetual motion machine. Just as the three years of labor, precious metals and exotic woods that went into their creation might have been put to better use if he had been schooled in the most basic precepts of physics, a modicum of knowledge of world events could counter what ignorance has done to "this whole ruined planet" (14).

Hocus Pocus is a Vonnegut novel proper. Its concerns are consistent with Vonnegut's focus since *Player Piano*. Automation and lack of usefulness breeds apathy. Little things, like Hartke's scraps of paper that are the medium of the novel, are the chance events that determine life. Hartke finds himself at the mercy of someone else's created fiction, namely his commanding officers, who force him to spin the losses of the Vietnam War into successes. "I was a genius of lethal *Hocus Pocus!*" he says of his wartime justifications (154). There aren't any villains, or at least, as Vonnegut has noted before, they aren't people. "The biggest character in *Hocus Pocus* (excluding myself of course)," writes Vonnegut in his special preface to the book's Franklin Library edition, "is imperialism, the capture of other societies' lands and people and treasure by means of state-of-the-art wounding and killing machines, which is to say armies and navies" (*Fates* 130). So, too, is Eugene Debs Hartke a narrator like Karebekian, Starbuck, and Waltz and even Leon Trotsky Trout, who looks back over his life from a prison whether literal or figurative, deciding whether or not to issue a *mea culpa* on his life. While these narrators find their destinies to be (like Darwinian evolution) combinations of chance and genetic or biochemical predisposition, the act of recalling affects a change or resignation on the part of the viewpoint character. Here, Hartke moves closer as the novel unfolds from his murderous, womanizing past to something more like his namesakes, repeat presidential candidate Eugene V. Debs and outspoken Vietnam detractor Senator Vance Hartke.

Vonnegut's glimpse of America in 2001 is one of his most gruesome projections. The novel ends with Hartke in jail awaiting his trial for masterminding the jailbreak, wrongly accused. Of the few positives Vonnegut allows to come out of the story are Hartke's understanding of the buffoonery that has created his current environment, and the fact that he is qualified as a spokesman to point out society's foolhardiness in court.

Perhaps due to Vonnegut's insistence that writing is good therapy, he was able to resume his tour on the college lecture circuit after the publication of *Hocus Pocus. Fates Worse Than Death*, his second "autobiographical collage," appeared just one year later in 1991. Like *Wampeters* and *Palm Sunday* it reprints his most telling and harder to access essays, though *Fates* is heavier on connecting material than was its forbear *Palm Sunday*. It addresses some of his most personal events, including his own suicide attempt in 1984.

Vonnegut had grown increasingly tiresome of writing after *Hocus Pocus*, and for years he wrestled with his fourteenth novel, *Timequake*, giving up on it several times in the six years between *Fates* and its publication.

During this time Vonnegut worked on his silkscreen art with Lexington-based artist Joe Petro III. Their collaboration for an Absolut vodka advertisement began as a joke, but Petro encouraged Vonnegut to continue. He had already a predisposition to create art: he drew in his books occasionally since *Slaughterhouse-Five*; his father and grandfather had both turned to painting later in life; his sister and several of his children showed both promise and realization as artists. He produces silkscreens to this day in collaboration with Petro, selling prints of his work on the website, www.vonnegut.com. The hobby for Vonnegut, writes Klinkowitz, "would occupy his future while once more gathering purpose from his past" (*Vonnegut in Fact*, 8).

By 1996 he had trashed the reluctantly nascent *Timequake* yet again. He told the *Denver Post* during a benefit featuring his prints for the Denver Public Library, "I spent four years working on another novel for Putnam. It was called *Timequake,* but I didn't like it, so I dropped it. I don't plan to go out with a piece of —" (September 14, 1996). The same article mentions that he's working on his memoir, and it is perhaps most indicative of Vonnegut's predilection toward experiment that by 1997 the two would be combined into his most unorthodox novel yet.

TIMEQUAKE

"This is an experiment that I'm performing in my head and it turns out to be *so* complicated that to do it justice, after farting around with it, the responsibilities that I've saddled myself with are just enormous" (Reed and Leeds 38).

The premise is that for reasons unknown on February 13, 2001, the universe stopped expanding and instead, collapsed a distance of ten years, sending the entire world back in time to whatever they were doing on February 21, 1991. Everyone has to live every moment of the last ten years over again, unable to do anything differently, unable to say anything differently, unable even to know if this is happening to anyone else but themselves.

As he has lamented in the past, and as he explains in the prologue, the novel would not work. Reaching his seventy-fourth birthday, he opted to dissect the best parts of the story and mix them like a "stew" with his own thoughts and reminiscences, the tenor of which is much like his prose in *Fates Worse Than Death*. The resulting book is something only Vonnegut could get away with: bits of memoirs with a novel running through them, and a fantastic novel at that. Vonnegut takes part in the timequake too, taking care to "count the rerun" in his reminiscences. He records conversations between himself and Kilgore Trout, who is, of course, a fiction. In this sense he is more involved in *Timequake* than in any of his previous works, save perhaps *Slaughterhouse-Five*.

The result of living ten years of life over again is that everyone is "on autopilot" when "free will" kicks in again. People have become so much the passive observers of their own lives that no one thinks to be agents in their lives. The consequences are on the level of a Vonnegutian cataclysm. First, millions of people fell down, "because the weight on their feet had been unevenly distributed when free will kicked in" (*Timequake*, 105); but "the real mayhem" was caused by planes, trucks, cars, and other "self-propelled forms of transportation," whose pilots expected the vehicle to fly or drive itself, like it had for ten years.

Kilgore Trout gets much of the fictional happenings in *Timequake*, as the eighty-four-year old still writing bad science fiction with a purpose. Vonnegut gets to chat with him at a clambake taking place in the writer's colony called Xanadu after time catches up with itself; these conversations and his paraphrased short stories, as usual, supply much of the commentary, though it is liable to come from anywhere.

Timequake features many of Trout's stories, which, as they have always been, are hyperbolic science fiction tales where allegory is far more important than the story itself. Vonnegut remarks on their origin, saying, "I still think up short stories from time to time, as though there were money in it. The habit dies hard.... All I do with short stories ideas now is rough them out, credit them to Kilgore Trout, and put them in a novel" (15). This explains their brevity and poor development—characteristics which have long been the charm of Trout's fiction. Trout's jeremiad to a fellow bum who suggests he might make money with his stories at the American Academy of Arts and Letters, which neighbor his homeless shelter, is easily synecdochic of Vonnegut's larger career:

> "If I'd wasted my time creating characters," Trout said, "I would never have gotten around to calling attention to things that really matter: irresistible forces of nature, and cruel inventions, and cockamamie ideals and governments and economies that make heroes and heroines alike feel like something the cat drug in."

To which Vonnegut adds:

> Trout might have said, and it can be said of me as well, that he created *caricatures* rather than characters. His animus against so-called *mainstream literature*, moreover, wasn't peculiar to him. It was generic among writers of science fiction. (63)

Trout, the first to understand what had happened when the rerun is over, has the task of rousing everyone into willfulness again. Not everyone is happy about the prospect of making choices in an absurd, unpredictable universe again. "You know what you can do with free will?" asks Dudley Prince, an African-American who served seven years of hard time framed for the rape and murder of a ten-year-old. "You can stuff it up your ass" (167).

Still, because of the chaos of cars and trucks crashing into buildings, and planes that are truly "on autopilot" running out of fuel, the senior citizen Trout must set humanity into action again. His magic words to break people from their trance are "You were sick, but now you're well, and there's work to do" (167). Thus Trout in allegory plays the role Vonnegut has made for himself in his career: the world is destroying itself around him, and Vonnegut must find the right words to break the apathy of the rest of the world.

On this account, Vonnegut takes every opportunity to editorialize in *Timequake,* still creating melancholy but humorous invectives against his lifelong nemeses. Of America's continued continued love-affair with weapons he writes: "That there are such devices as firearms, as easy to operate as cigarette lighters and as cheap as toasters, capable at anybody's whim of killing Father or Fats [Waller] or Abraham Lincoln or John Lennon or Martin Luther King, Jr., or a woman pushing a baby carriage, should be proof enough for anybody that, to quote the old science fiction writer Kilgore Trout, 'being alive is a crock of shit'" (2-3). He postulates that "we poison the water and air and topsoil, and construct ever more cunning doomsday devices" because, and here he quotes Thoreau, "'the mass of men lead lives of quiet desperation.'" His pessimism is unrelenting: "For practically everybody, the end of the world can't come soon enough" (2).

It is clear from Trout's story, "The Sisters of B-36," that Vonnegut's latter-day Luddism had not faded in the wake of the digitization of America in the 1990's. Two of the three sisters are artists that write short stories and paint paintings important to the development of the imaginations of young Booboolings, inhabitants of the planet Booboo—the big brains of young Booboolings become programmed to imagine and to behave appropriately by growing circuits in response to their art. The third sister, a scientist who learned calculus and thermodynamics from lunatics in an asylum she played in as a child, became jealous of her sisters' popularity, and so she invented and marketed television to make her sisters feel "like something the cat drug in." Television became extremely popular, and "[y]oung Booboolings didn't see any point in developing imaginations anymore, since all they had to do was turn on a switch and see all kinds of jazzy shit." The scientist succeeded in breaking her sister's spirits but the bad sister was still unpopular and boring, so she goes on to develop cars and computers and weapons of war. The resulting lack of imagination and human contact makes Booboolings "among the most merciless creatures in the local family of galaxies" (17–18).

For Vonnegut, community is among the most important facets of a tolerable human life, and the malevolence of television has as much to do with its ability to put us in complacent loneliness as its bane to the imagination. Plays, he says, evoke so much emotional and ethical force because of the conviviality of the audience. The plays he encountered in his youth have as much impact on him today because "I was immobilized in a congregation of rapt fellow human beings in a theatre when I first saw and heard them. They would have made no more of an impression on me than *Monday Night Football*, had I been alone eating nachos and gazing into the face of a cathode-ray tube" (22). Television isolates people from each other, bearing directly on our emotional capacity.

The rise of computers—and their conspicuous movement to ever smaller, less conspicuous sizes (from the monstrosity of EPICAC in Vonnegut's *Player Piano* to the tiny microchip)—only bolsters his contention in his first novel that technology comes at the expense of human dignity. Architect Frank Pepper commits suicide when a computer program called Palladio designs an implausible three-story parking garage in thirty minutes. After Frank's death, his brother Zoltan asks, "Why is it so important that we all be humiliated, with such ingenuity and at such great expense? We never thought we were such hot stuff in the first place" (45).

He continues his diatribe against capitalism:

Why throw money at problems? That is what money is for.

Should the nation's wealth be redistributed? It has and continues to be redistributed to a few people in a manner strikingly unhelpful. (163–164)

Interspersed in *Timequake* are solutions for improvement in the form of new amendments to the Constitution. The four are codifications of so much he has written over fifty years, especially economic inequity, and the role of the individual in the larger community.

> Article XXVII: Every newborn shall be sincerely welcomed and cared for until maturity.
> Article XXIX: Every adult who needs it shall be given meaningful work to do, at a living wage.
> Article XXX: Every person, upon reaching a statutory age of puberty, shall be declared an adult in a solemn public ritual, during which he or she must welcome his or her new responsibilities in the community, and their attendant dignities.
> Article XXXI: Every effort shall be made to make every person feel that he or she will be sorely missed when he or she is gone. (152, 175)

"Such essential elements in an ideal diet for human spirit, of course," Vonnegut adds, "can be provided convincingly only by extended families" (175).

The last Article is indicative of Vonnegut's sense that his life is nearly over in the summer of 1996, when much of the personal and editorial content for the book was written. At the clambake in Xanadu, Vonnegut gathers his old family, friends, and associates, living or dead, real or not. The attendees are not there to see him, but his invocation of so many figures from his life is clearly his goodbye. Vonnegut had considered *Timequake* his last book, saying so even in the prologue. Valerie Sayers' gratified review in the *New York Times* notes it "was obviously inspired by a sense that his life's work was winding down" (Sayers 14). Vonnegut has started another novel since titled "If God Were Alive Today." He remarked on why he began another novel after he made it clear that *Timequake* was his adieu. "I didn't know. I thought I was going to die" (Abel, 1).

The gathering at Xanadu is a funeral of a kind, however. The pretext is a cast party for the production of *Abe Lincoln in Illinois*, and those present "were mourning not only Lincoln, but the death of American *eloquence*" (204). Lincoln's farewell speech is recorded in the book, and it moves the audience so much that the curmudgeonly Kilgore Trout sobs at its beauty.

That it is a funeral is in keeping with *Timequake's* one great leitmotif, memory. The vivid recollections of Vonnegut's beloved family members, of his sister Alice and his brother Bernard, who had recently passed at the time of *Timequake's* authoring, of his influential Uncle Alex, of his mother in her fatal materialism and his father in his art-centered eccentricity, haunt the novel, break up the narrative, and make it obvious that they are "sorely missed."

Even though *Timequake* was Vonnegut's last novel, his name continued to appear in review columns. His friend and critic Peter Reed collected twenty-three shorter works from Vonnegut's early career in *Bagombo Snuff Box* (1999). The same year, Seven Stories Press printed *God Bless You, Dr. Kevorkian*, a light-hearted collection of twenty-one "interviews" the author conducted in Heaven with the departed, including such figures as Isaac Newton and Adolf Hitler with the lesser-known, like Harold Epstein and Peter Pellegrino, whose fervent loves of gardening and hot-air ballooning exemplify earthly happiness. The interviews were originally radio spots for WNYC, the Manhattan Public Radio station, and proceeds from the book benefited that organization. "It does what no commercial TV or radio station can afford to do anymore," Vonnegut wrote in the introduction. WNYC satisfies people's right to know—as contrasted with, as abject slaves of high-roller publicists and advertisers, keeping the public vacantly diverted and entertained" (12).

Vonnegut survived a cigarette-sparked house fire on Superbowl Sunday in 2000—getting away with smoke inhalation after the onetime volunteer firefighter tried to extinguish the blaze himself. In 2001 he taught creative writing at Smith College in Northampton, Massachusetts, while he continued work on "If God Were Alive Today." He was also named State Author for New York. The novel remains in-progress, and until its publication, we may look forward to the work of countless young writers he has inspired with his novels and teaching. When a Smith undergraduate had Vonnegut critique her short story, which she described as "a heartwarming account of her grandmother's death," he suggested it was too gushy, and offered, "have you ever thought of making your grandmother insane?"

CHAPTER EIGHT

The Man with
Something to Say

*A Vonnegut book is not cute or precious. It is
literally awful, for Vonnegut is one of the few writers
able to lift the lid of the garbage can, and
dispassionately examine the contents....*

—J. Michael Crichton, *New Republic*

KURT VONNEGUT WROTE HIMSELF into American literature and
history over the course of the second half of the last century, both
with what he had to say and how he said it. There is a consistency
in his messages, a bevy of recurring themes, and an uncanny
writing style spanning his canon, in spite of how various his works
may be.

Perhaps because of the overwhelming success of *Slaughterhouse-
Five*, with its aliens and time travel, elements of the fantastic in
Vonnegut's work have been extant in the eyes of readers. Especially
earlier in his writing, there was a need to defend against attempts
to label Vonnegut a writer of science fiction. Over the years,
though, the author and his critics have demonstrated that the
fantastic in his novels is secondary to the text.

Vonnegut himself has likened the extraordinary moments in his
books to Shakespeare's use of clowns—part of an effort to lighten

the reader after a bleak or morose turn. Here is the humorist in Vonnegut.

Commonly, though, the science fiction backdrops function as props used by the author to make his statement on the human condition. Dan Wakefield made the contrast between Vonnegut's craft and the genre of science fiction succinctly in *The Vonnegut Statement*. Wakefield is not a fan of the fantastic:

> By that I mean I don't like books that have green monsters with five arms, and lost tribes that are ruled by electronic lizards.
>
> But Vonnegut's "science-fiction" wasn't like that at all. It was about people, doing things that people might do if things had turned out just a little bit differently; or maybe if we *knew* more about what was really going on. (Klinkowitz and Somer 62)

The other-worldly gives Vonnegut a chance to show what is happening here in ours; it is a way of exposing (negative) influences that might make things "turn out a little differently," or a means of pointing out "what is really going on." Peter J. Reed notes the utility of his style, saying that "the fantastic offers perception into the quotidian, rather than escape from it" (Reed, *Fantastic Faces* 77). If Vonnegut didn't appear to be having so much fun using fantasy in his books, one almost senses that he includes these elements grudgingly—as if his message necessitates the form.

This method and purpose in light of a rather timely iconoclasm places his fiction squarely in the realm of satire. Like other great satirists, he rails against perceived wrongs and insouciances of society around him. Some of the earliest academic criticism he received set him in a tradition with the likes of Jonathan Swift and Voltaire. "His novels have something of Swift in them," wrote Jerry Bryant in his 1970 survey of contemporary literature, "not merely in the canny pokes he takes at human weakness and the status quo, but a kind of fantasy that allows him, as it allowed Swift, to isolate the objects of his attack and praise" (Bryant, 303).

In literary history, though, Vonnegut has expressed an affinity, above all, to the man after whom he named his first-born: Mark Twain. Twain's name was invoked conspicuously by Granville Hicks in his 1969 treatment of *Slaughterhouse-Five* in the *Saturday Review*. At the time of Hicks' review, Vonnegut was known (if at all) to be a science fiction writer with a cult following in regular consumers of that genre, and in the particularly youthful collegiate crowd. Hicks told his literary audience of his delight hearing Vonnegut speak a year earlier at Notre Dame, "as funny a lecture as I had ever listened to." He asked his readers to look beyond the science fiction superficies of Vonnegut's previous works. "What he really is," Hicks wrote, "is a sardonic humorist and satirist in the vein of Mark Twain and Jonathan Swift." He added that, like Twain, "Vonnegut feels sadness as well as indignation when he looks at the damned human race" (Hicks 25).

Klinkowitz reports the breakthrough in *Vonnegut In Fact*:

> Science fiction, Hicks realized, was at least a tangential concern in the author's earlier work: *Player Piano, Cat's Cradle*, and *God Bless You, Mr. Rosewater* had made great fun of the worship of science and technology; misfunctions of both were responsible for catastrophes of plot and hilarities of incident, not to mention a dim overview of human strivings toward a mechanical ideal. (*Vonnegut In Fact* 11–12)

For his own part, Vonnegut speaks of Twain's writings as a childhood influence. Twain "encouraged me when I was young to believe that there was so much that was amusing and beautiful on this continent that I need not be awed by persons from anywhere else" (*Palm Sunday*, 166). Vonnegut was asked to speak at an event celebrating the centennial of the completion of Mark Twain's Connecticut home, he said, because, like Twain, he is "simultaneously a humorist and serious novelist" (166). He told those attending that Twain galvanized his atheism: "I was confirmed in my skepticism by Mark Twain during my formative years, and by some other good people, too," adding that he, like Twain, will be bitter in his later years, because "I will finally realize that I had it right all along: that I will not see God, that there is no heaven or Judgment Day" (168). In the speech, Twain's "innocent joking about technology and superstition" in *A Connecticut Yankee in King Arthur's Court* is shown to be much like Vonnegut's work. Twain's story has the Yankee and a few dozen other men take their modern technology to the Dark Ages, killing twenty-five thousand armed attackers with Gatling guns in the space of ten minutes. Having reminded the audience that this story was supposed to be funny, Vonnegut points out that such a "lark" was sadly prescient of the First World War (169–171).

Vonnegut has also been an active public speaker, and, like Twain, is unafraid to take up advocacy in those venues. His attitude toward the role of the writer, in fact, demanded it:

> My motives are political. I agree with Stalin and Hitler and Mussolini that the writer should serve his society. I differ with dictators as to how writers should serve. Mainly, they should be— and biologically have to be—agents of change. For the better, we hope. (76)

He talked about the author's role as a speaker in the preface to *Wampeters, Foma, and Granfalloons* (1974): "I do think...that public speaking is almost the only way a poet or a novelist or a playwright can have any political effectiveness in his creative prime. If he tries to put his politics into a work of the imagination, he will foul up his work beyond all recognition" (*Wampeters*, xiv). Public speaking, then, in light of his motivation for writing, was inevitable. It is simply the most effective way he can influence society. Jerome Klinkowitz once reminded Vonnegut in a letter that Granville Hicks' review, which was so important in introducing the author to the literary establishment, came after Hicks had seen and enjoyed Vonnegut's lecture at Notre Dame a year before. Vonnegut wrote back: "It really makes a difference, I find, if people hear me speak" (Reed and Leeds 59–60).

Of course, Vonnegut *would* find ways after he wrote those words to advance more views in his novels without "foul[ing] up his work beyond all recognition," editorializing more and speaking less with age. In public appearances, though, he was able to speak to the point, advancing his progressive vision. He finished a 1970 commencement speech at Bennington College with a plain advocacy of socialism:

> So let's divide up the wealth of the world more fairly than we have divided it up so far. Let's make sure that everybody has enough to eat, and a decent place to live, and medical help when he needs it. Let's stop spending money on weapons, which don't work anyway, thank God, and spend money on each other. It isn't moonbeams to talk of modest plenty for all. They have it in Sweden. We can have it here. Dwight David Eisenhower once pointed out that Sweden, with its many Utopian programs, had a high rate of alcoholism and suicide and youthful unrest. Even so, I would like to see America try socialism. If we start drinking heavily and killing ourselves, and if our children start acting crazy, we can go back to good old Free Enterprise again. (*Wampeters*, 170)

The above is not exceptional in content for the myriad public speeches Vonnegut has given over the past few decades. Jerome Klinkowitz has written most extensively of Vonnegut in this role, linking the author's dynamism in front of an audience with that in his books:

> With an audience present, one can witness Vonnegut's proposing and responding, acting and reacting, drawing on his own experience to meld it with the experiences of his listeners in order to produce a work that succeeds as performance. It is an analog to what he accomplishes on the printed page, where the same living presence engages a subject matter that is part historical and part fabrication, but which in combination becomes an action painting with words. (Reed and Leeds 71)

Vonnegut lines up on the left in all his views. "If there's a liberal cause," David Streitfeld wrote in the *Washington Post* in 1991, "he's willing, cigarette in hand, to lend his support" (Streitfeld c.01). Yet despite the perception of Vonnegut as a radical, he

THE MAN WITH SOMETHING TO SAY ■ 125

protests that his beliefs stem from anything but old-fashioned American values. He told *Playboy* that "everything I believe I was taught in junior civics during the Great Depression— at School 43 in Indianapolis, with full approval of the school board" (*Conversations* 103). His pacifism, he points out, was the attitude of the entire, isolationist nation before America was made to enter World War II, and he holds the Germans and the Japanese accountable for forcing America to take up arms. He fights against American reluctance to lessen its standing army, to disarm: America should wane to a nation that does not consider war inevitable. Building and maintaining nuclear weapons is especially ridiculous.

He relates in the prologue to *Jailbird* that he cast ballots for the Socialist ticket the first time he voted in a national election. "I believed that socialism would be good for the common man. As a private first class in the infantry, I was surely a common man" (*Jailbird*, xii). Vonnegut's socialism is an extension of his interest in the plight of the worker and the labor movement in America. The technological advancements he witnessed first-hand at General Electric, too, gave him insight into a world where people were rapidly being replaced by machines, and where environmental concerns were a concession to progress. There is a strong correlative, for Vonnegut, between dignity and meaningful work; he saw this in his own life as his father's sense of worth was diminished over the ten years he went without a commission. A structured, socialist atmosphere where work is provided for those who want it would augment dignity, at least.

With so much in Vonnegut's view to be changed—and with a good deal of urgency, too—it is unsurprising that he looks on the world with pessimism. Harry Reasoner cornered Vonnegut as a pessimist in a 1969 interview. Vonnegut answered, "Well, things do seem to get worse" (*Conversations* 17).

His grim presentation, though, is an important part of his message. Painting a disaster doesn't do any good if people don't feel bad after seeing it. Vonnegut says that *Dr. Strangelove*, for example, "sent people home utterly satisfied." "I'm sure that everyone that ever sees that picture sleeps soundly afterward and feels nothing more ever needs to be done" (*Conversations* 235). In contrast, Harold Bloom remembers his "shocked admiration" for *Slaughterhouse-Five* on his first read—"a very disturbing and disturbed book," that he was "not looking forward to encountering again" (Bloom 1).

We may add to the Vonnegutian preoccupations of war, socioeconomics, and environmentalism that of mental illness. Frequently, Vonnegut's protagonists are depressed and even certifiably insane. Suicides abound. Vonnegut has explained the prevalence by citing it as a very real fact of human experience—his own experiences with depression, his mother's suicide, and his son Mark's battle with manic depression have informed this view. And since he feels that mental instability has everything to do with our inherited chemical compositions, insanity, too, is a matter of fate.

Lawrence Broer's *Sanity Plea: Schizophrenia in the Novels of Kurt Vonnegut* points out that "there actually comes a moment in every Vonnegut novel when the hero is driven to or over the edge of insanity—when contrasts between the world as orderly, rational, and humane and the world as a slaughterhouse of ongoing violence and cruelty become too unbalancing to endure" (Broer 6). Broer's book actually presents the well-supported opinion that Vonnegut's novels are not altogether pessimistic and fatalist—that those attitudes are just one side of the schizoid nature of Vonnegut's characters, who are split between the "self that affirms" and the "self that denies." "In one novel after another, we witness the sometimes despairing, sometimes hopeful efforts of Vonnegut's fragmented protagonists to put their disintegrated selves together again—to resist the various forms of moral escapism that paralyze their creative will and to achieve a wholeness of spirit" (Broer 10-11). The central concern of every one of Vonnegut's novels, according to Broer, is whether the character will reconcile the dichotomy of his ego, half of which has a will to be.

In terms of a more generalized wretchedness—the sort of poor mental health experienced by characters in his novels largely from *Slapstick* on—the diminished mental and emotional self is a symptom of the loss of a supportive family. Following his instruction in anthropology at the University of Chicago, he came to the conclusion that our biology makes us want to live in the intimate, sharing groups of people living in an extended family expounded by Dr. Robert Redfield. "[W]e are full of chemicals which require us to belong to folk societies," Vonnegut told the National Institute of Arts and Letters, "or failing that, to feel lousy all the time" (*Wampeters* 180). He concluded an address to the American Psychiatric Association as follows:

> All of you, I am sure, when writing a prescription for mildly depressed patients, people nowhere as sick as my mother or my son were, have had a thought on this order: "I am so sorry to have to put you on the outside of a pill. I would give anything if I could put you inside the big, warm life support system of an extended family instead." (*Fates* 35)

Thus Eliot Rosewater's insanity is, if not cured, at least reconciled by his legal adoption of all who claim to be his offspring; and Karebekian's depressive loneliness is alleviated by an artificial family in his household. That Vonnegut feels the bulk of American anxieties stem from sheer loneliness cannot be overstated. Vonnegut seems to accept, though, that the close extended family is irrecoverable in America. He will settle for artificial systems of support—or even simple acts of decency toward one another.

"I admire Christianity more than anything—Christianity as symbolized by gentle people sharing a common bowl" (*Conversations* 82). Except for the congregational environment of the church—which is adequate in his view as an artificial family—religions, with their attempts to make sense of the universe, are among the most ridiculous of mankind's ventures. The absurd, chaotic, random universe supercedes the possibility of a caring God. "I beg you to believe in the most ridiculous superstition of all," Vonnegut jibed in a 1970 commencement speech "that humanity is at the center of the universe, the fulfiller or the frustrator of the grandest dreams of God Almighty" (*Wampeters* 165). The notion that humans are of any concern to the universe is unfounded, and the anthropocentrism engendered by that belief is undeserving. "What could we do or say that could possibly interest Thee?" asks the Reverend C. Horner Redwine of the Church of God the Utterly Indifferent in *The Sirens of Titan* (*Sirens* 215).

In that book, Rumfoord proselytizes that humanity can be saved from those who claim to do the will of God by professing that God has no will. Chance, luck, accidents determine the course of life. That there is no meaning or causality in any event aligns Vonnegut with an existentialist school of thought: even though we might have the freedom to make choices, the absurd, meaningless universe makes any rational choice impossible.

Thanks to his fatalism, Vonnegut's pedigree is a great factor in his life and fiction. Most people feel that they could have been born elsewhere, and into different circumstances. Vonnegut has no trouble imagining how his life *might have been*. What if he was born a German, instead of a German-American? In his 1966 introduction to *Mother Night* (1961), about an American playwright living in Germany who is so engrossed in German culture he becomes a Nazi propagandist, he posits that, had his family remained in Germany, he "would have *been* a Nazi, bopping Jews and gypsies and Poles around, leaving boots sticking out of snowbanks, warming myself with my secretly virtuous insides" (*Mother Night* vii).

This has lent itself to a sensitivity of his German background. Robert Merrill reports that Vonnegut has only once directly identified himself as a German-American (Reed and Leeds 76). He once declined to testify on the atrocity of the Dresden massacre in a film because "I had a German name. I didn't want to argue with people who thought Dresden should have been bombed to hell" (Hayman et al. 70). He recollects this discomfort in his last novel, *Timequake* (1997):

> When I took a job in Boston as an advertising copywriter, because I was broke, an account executive asked me what kind of a name Vonnegut was. I said, "German." He said, "Germans killed six million of my cousins." (*Timequake* 42–43)

Vonnegut has sensed the host of connections his background implies, and the implications of this marginalization appear in his fiction. Merrill points out that in the earlier *Slaughterhouse-Five* and *Mother Night*, "Vonnegut works very hard to avoid trafficking in the more obvious stereotypes." *Mother Night*, for instance, features "a collection of American Nazis to balance their German counterparts." And *Slaughterhouse-Five* reserves the bulk of its critique for the Allied act of melting Dresden. "The Germans of *Slaughterhouse-Five* appear briefly, but collectively they constitute a very sympathetic human community—realistically diverse but marked by several genuine 'characters' and no villains" (Merrill 79–80).

Frequently, a character finds himself at odds with his heredity, born into circumstances he cannot control. This is especially true in Vonnegut's later works, where the problem in the novel is not imminent cataclysm, but internal guilt. Rudy Waltz of *Deadeye Dick* (who is demonstrably a personification of Vonnegut) has parents who resemble Vonnegut's in every way, except that his father wallows in his German heritage, even befriending Hitler in his youth and only withdrawing from the relationship when World War II makes it impossible. Rudy fails to overcome the guilt of his past. Only in his later novel *Bluebeard* does a protagonist (Rabo Karebekian) "overcome first the problems he inherits from his parents, then the mistakes he commits in compensating for his childhood" (Reed and Leeds 81).

In importance and frequency, the problematic nature of fiction features in his work as heavily as any other preoccupations. Repeatedly, Vonnegut shows that people try to imitate the unrealistic world of stories in reality. One result is the expectation that reality will behave like a story. Television is a prime culprit. This problem has only been amplified by the vast number of conflicts and (more importantly) resolutions we see on television everyday, to the extent that we expect the world to entertain us. *Playboy* asked the author to what he attributed the "spectacular failure" of the 1972 McGovern campaign against Richard Nixon:

He failed as an actor. He couldn't create on camera a character we could love or hate. So America voted to have his show taken off the air. The American audience doesn't care about an actor's private life, doesn't want his show continued simply because he's honorable and truthful and has the best interests of the nation at heart in private life. Only one thing matters: Can he jazz us up on camera? This is a national tragedy, of course—that we've changed from a society to an audience. And poor McGovern did what any actor would have done with a failing show. He blamed the scripts, junked a lot of his old material, which was actually beautiful, called for new material, which was actually old material that other performers had had some luck with. He probably couldn't have won, though, even if he had been Clark Gable. (*Conversations* 101–102)

Furthermore, people unwittingly try to fulfill these fictions. "We live more according to literary stereotypes and dramatic stereotypes than we know," (*Conversations* 234). Dr. Felix Hoenikker of *Cat's Cradle* was based on the General Electric research scientist Irving Langmuir, who fit the stereotype of the absent-minded scientist uncannily. Vonnegut claims that Langmuir and others permitted themselves to shun responsibility for the consequences of their discoveries because there were literary forbears for their roles. "I think there were literary models then of pure scientists and their absent-mindedness...and many scientists gladly fell into this stereotype of absent-mindedness and indifference, including indifference as to what became of their discoveries" (*Conversations* 234). Vonnegut is quick to point to the potential danger here; in *Cat's Cradle*, obviously, such permitted playfulness—based on a fictional model—allowed the development of the atomic bomb and the destruction of the world.

At least as far back as *Slaughterhouse-Five*, Vonnegut had noticed this tendency and sought to subvert it by specifically *not* creating tales with beginnings, middles, and ends. A passage from *Breakfast of Champions* where Vonnegut steps into the action is particularly evocative of his whole thought on the subject:

I thought Beatrice Keedsler [the novelist] had joined hands with other old-fashioned storytellers to make people believe that life had leading characters, minor characters, significant details, insignificant details, that it had lessons to be learned, tests to be passed, and a beginning, a middle, and an end.

As I approached my fiftieth birthday, I had become more and more enraged and mystified by the idiot decisions made by my countrymen. And then I had come suddenly to pity them, for I understood how innocent and natural it was for them to behave so abominably, and with such abominable results: They were doing their best to live like people invented in story books. This was the reason Americans shot each other so often: It was a convenient literary device for ending short stories and books.

Why were so many Americans treated by their government as though their lives were as disposable as paper facial tissues? Because that was the way authors customarily treated bit-part players in their made-up tales.

And so on.

Once I understood what was making America such a dangerous, unhappy nation of people who had nothing to do with real life, I resolved to shun storytelling. I would write about life. Every person would be exactly as important as every other. All facts would also be given equal weightiness. Nothing would be left out. Let others bring order to chaos. I would bring chaos to order, instead, which I think I have done. (*Breakfast of Champions*, 209–210)

He did. James Lundquist shows how:

In a major sense, Vonnegut's novels represent just such an adaptation. He moves steadily away from old-fashioned stories of the sort that lead readers to believe life has leading characters and minor characters, important details and unimportant details, lessons to be learned in order to pass tests of physical, psychological, or spiritual strength, beginnings, middles, ends. By the time Vonnegut gets to *Breakfast of Champions*, he has resolved to avoid storytelling in favor of a kind of writing in which all persons are equally important and the only moral is to adapt oneself to the requirements of chaos rather than to the requirements of an orderly universe (the most laughable and also the most fatal of illusions). (Lundquist 101)

In other words, the universe is chaotic, and to present it any other way is downright dangerous.

This narrative theory leads to much of what critics consider to be postmodern in Vonnegut's writing. In calling attention to the novel as an artifice, rather than a fiction put to the reader as truth, Vonnegut subverts the text itself, alerting the reader of its contrived, unreal nature. But Vonnegut has too much to say to be a postmodernist proper. He offers solutions to the bleakness described in his novels: the big family, for one. As David Cowart has it, even if those solutions are unrealistic or unworkable, it is at least a try.

...the attempt to promote such a meliorist fiction reveals once again the humane sanity that has always distinguished Vonnegut and his work. It reveals a principled resistance to the nihilistic seductions of postmodernism, which more and more contemporary novelists have instinctively or consciously recognized as a moral and aesthetic dead end. (Merrill 186)

Cowart concludes that because Vonnegut insists on bringing meanings and morals into his fiction while utilizing postmodern devices like black humor, linguistic determination, and self-reflexivity, he spans modernism and postmodernism. "Vonnegut plays the game, but he also hangs on to the ideas of meaning and value" (186).

Ironically, Vonnegut's career reads the like rise, fall, and redemption of the Cinderella story he has worked to discount in his novels. He wrote in relative obscurity in the fifties, taking odd jobs, teaching positions, and paperback contracts for the money to support his family. Vonnegut remembered in *Timequake* that when a reporter once asked his son Mark "what it had been like to grow up with a famous father." He answered, "When I was growing up, my father was a car salesman who couldn't get a job teaching at Cape Cod Junior College" (*Timequake* 14).

Then one day in Boston a fairy godmother named Sam Lawrence gave him an invitation to the ball. Rising to national recognition in the 1960s, he became, in the words of the *Village Voice*, "an unexpected 'paperback writer' (in the old Beatles tune) who magically arose from the supermarket stalls to something like secular sainthood for 10 years or so" (Krim 81). In the seventies, when the clock struck midnight, *Breakfast of Champions*—and especially *Slapstick*—constituted a fall, in spirit anyway. Vonnegut's atonement in *Jailbird* and the five novels following are probably as close to happily ever after as he wants to get. He made the glass slipper fit. He lives on, writing and drawing indefinitely. "If God Were Alive Today," a novel-in-progress, is no doubt awaited by many.

But this, too, is an attempt to turn life into a fiction. An existence graphed solely on the critical success of his books he has written leaves out precisely the subject he has been writing about: humanity. The tragedies and fortunes Vonnegut has lived, especially since he has tendered so many intimate, autobiographical details, are a necessary part of his message on the human condition.

Abel, David. "So It Goes for Vonnegut at Smith, 78-Year-Old Author Still Shaking Up the Establishment." *The Boston Globe*. May 5, 2001: 1.

Allen, W.R., ed. *Conversations with Kurt Vonnegut*. Jackson: University Press of Mississippi, 1988.

———. *Understanding Kurt Vonnegut*. Columbia, South Carolina: University of South Carolina Press, 1991.

Anderson, Lisa. "Vonnegut's vision 'I had such high hopes for the planet ... after everyone had sacrificed so much and behaved so well'" *Chicago Tribune*. September 2, 1990: 1.

Bloom, H., ed. *Kurt Vonnegut's Slaughterhouse-Five*. Modern Critical Interpretations. Philadelphia: Chelsea House Publishers, 2001.

Broer, L.R. *Sanity Plea: Schizophrenia in the Novels of Kurt Vonnegut*. Tuscaloosa: University of Alabama Press, 1989.

Bryant, J.H. *The Open Decision: The Contemporary American Novel and Its Intellectual Background*. New York: Free Press, 1970.

Crichton, J. Michael. "Sci-Fi and Vonnegut." *The New Republic*. April 26, 1969: 33–35.

"The Devil's Work." Anonymous. *New York Times*. November 17, 1973.

Giannone, R. *Vonnegut: A Preface to His Novels*. Port Washington: Kennikat Press, 1977.

Hassan, Ihab. *Liberations*. Middletown, Conn.: Wesleyan University Press 1971.

Hayman, D., D. Michaelis, et al. "The Art of Fiction LXIV." *The Paris Review* 69:55–103, 1977.

Hicks, G. "Literary Horizons." *Saturday Review*. March 29, 1969: 25.

Hill, Gladwin. "Ten Cities Bombed" *New York Times*. February 15, 1945.

Klinkowitz, J. and J. Somer, eds. *The Vonnegut Statement*. New York: Delacorte Press, 1973.

Klinkowitz, J. and D.L. Lawler, eds. *Vonnegut in America : An Introduction to the Life and Work of Kurt Vonnegut.* New York: Delacorte Press, 1977.

Klinkowitz, J. *Kurt Vonnegut.* New York: Methuen & Co, 1982.

———. *Vonnegut in Fact: The Public Spokesmanship of Personal Fiction.* Columbia, South Carolina: University of South Carolina Press, 1998.

Kramer, Carol. "Kurt's College Cult Adopts Him as Literary Guru at 48." *Chicago Tribune.* November 15, 1970: 5.1.

Krim, S. "*Jailbird* Review" *The Village Voice.* New York: August 20, 1979: 81–82..

Lehmann-Haupt, Christopher. *New York Times* review. March 31, 1969.

Leonard, J. "Black Magic." *The Nation.* 251: 421–425, 1990.

Levin, Martin. "Do Human Beings Matter?: *God Bless You, Mr. Rosewater.* Or Pearls Before Swine." *New York Times.* April 25, 1965.

Lundquist, J. *Kurt Vonnegut.* New York: Ungar, 1977.

Mayo, C. *Kurt Vonnegut : The Gospel from Outer Space : (or, Yes We Have No Nirvanas).* San Bernadino, California: Borgo Press, 1977.

Merrill, R., ed. *Critical Essays on Kurt Vonnegut.* Boston: G.K. Hall & Co, 1990.

Reed, P.J. *Kurt Vonnegut, Jr.* New York: Thomas Y. Crowell Co, 1972.

———. *The Short Fiction of Kurt Vonnegut.* Westport, Conn.: Greenwood Press, 1997.

———. Kurt Vonnegut's Fantastic Faces. *Journal of the Fantastic in the Arts* 10, 1999.

Reed, P. J. and M. Leeds, eds. *The Vonnegut Chronicles: Interviews and Essays.* Contributions to the Study of World Literature. Westport, Connecticut: Greenwood Press, 1996.

Sale, Roger. "Kurt Vonnegut: writing with interchangeable parts." *New York Times.* October 3, 1976.

Sayers, Valerie. "Vonnegut Stew." *New York Times.* September 28, 1997.

Schatt, S. *Kurt Vonnegut, Jr.* Boston: Twayne Publishers, 1976.

Scholes, Robert. "Slapstick." Letter to the Editor. New York Times. November 21, 1976.

Seed, D. *Mankind Vs. Machines: The Technological Dystopia in Vonnegut's Player Piano.* Impossibility Fiction: Alternativity, Extrapolation, Speculation. D. Littlewood and P. Stockwell. Amsterdam ; Atlanta, GA: Rodopi. 17: 211, 1996.

Short, R. *Something to Believe In: Is Kurt Vonnegut the Exorcist or Jesus Christ Superstar?* San Francisco: Harper & Row, Publishers, 1978.

Streitfeld, David. "Vonnegut, From Cradle To Grave; The Writer and Failed Suicide, On the Fate of Survival. *The Washington Post.* August 29, 1991: c. 01.

Tanner, T. "The Uncertain Messenger: A Study of the Novels of Kurt Vonnegut," Jr. *Critical Quarterly* 11: 297–315, 1969.

Vonnegut, Kurt. "Speaking of Books: Science Fiction." *New York Times.* September 5, 1965.

———. *New York Times.* October 6, 1985.

———. Letter to the Editor. *New York Times.* March 27, 1991.

———. "Something's Rotten." *New York Times.* April 11, 1991.

———. "Venture for Vonnegut: Visual Art Novelist, 73, got his start on vodka ad Article 1 of 2 found." *Denver Post.* September 14, 1996.

Whitlark, J. *Vonnegut's Anthropology Thesis.* Literature and Anthropology. P. Dennis and W. Aycock. Lubbock: Texas Tech University Press, 1989.

Wright, Robert A. "Broad Spectrum of Writers Attacks Obscenity Ruling." *New York Times.* August 21, 1973.

Wood, Michael "Vonnegut's Softer Focus.". *New York Times* Review. September 9, 1979.

1848 Clemens Vonnegut, Sr., emigrates to America from Germany.

1913 On November 22, Clemens Vonnegut's grandson, Kurt Vonnegut, marries Edith Lieber in Indianapolis.

1922 Kurt Vonnegut, Jr. is born on November 11.

1940 Graduates from Shortridge High School, Indianapolis; he works as a columnist, reporter, and editor for the *Shortridge Daily Echo*, one of the first daily student newspapers in the country; enrolls at Cornell University as a chemistry major; he writes columns for the *Cornell Sun*.

1942 Enlists in the Army after his sophomore year.

1944 Granted leave in May to return to Indianapolis to visit his ailing mother, who commits suicide the day before he arrives.

1944–1945 Reaches the front in November as a battalion scout with the 106th infantry; Vonnegut is captured during the Battle of the Bulge; he works in a vitamin factory in Dresden, Germany.

1945 Dresden is firebombed by U.S. and British forces on February 13–14, leaving at least 35,000 inhabitants dead; Vonnegut survives in an underground meat locker; he is liberated in April when Soviet troops take Dresden; he returns to Indianapolis with a Purple Heart; marries Jane Marie Cox on September 1; in December, Vonnegut enrolls in the anthropology program at the University of Chicago.

1946 Works as a police reporter for the Chicago City News Bureau.

1947 Master's Thesis, *Fluctuations Between Good and Evil in Simple Tales* is unanimously rejected by University of Chicago; moves to Schenectady, New York, to work for General Electric in publicity; son Mark is born.

1950 On February 11, *Collier's* publishes Vonnegut's short story, "Report on the Barnhouse Effect."

1951	Resigns from General Electric to write full-time; he moves to Cape Cod, Massachusetts.
1952	*Player Piano*, Vonnegut's first novel, is published in paperback by Charles Scribner's Sons.
1952–1958	Short stories appear frequently in popular magazines.
1954	*Player Piano* is republished in paperback by Bantam as *Utopia 14*; attempts a variety of jobs including teaching and opening a Saab dealership; daughter Nanette is born.
1957	*Collier's* ceases publication; on October 1, Vonnegut's father dies.
1958	Vonnegut's sister Alice dies of cancer the day after her husband dies in a train crash. Kurt and Jane adopt their three oldest children (Tiger, Jim, and Steven).
1959	*The Sirens of Titan* is published in paperback by Dell.
1961	*Canary in a Cat House* is published in paperback by Fawcett; *The Sirens of Titan* is reissued in hardcover.
1962	*Mother Night* is published in paperback by Fawcett.
1963	*Cat's Cradle* is published by Holt, Rinehart and Winston.
1965	*God Bless You, Mr. Rosewater* is published by Holt, Rinehart and Winston; begins teaching in the Writers Workshop at the University of Iowa; writes first review for the *New York Times*.
1966	Hardcover edition of *Mother Night* is published, for which Vonnegut writes a new introduction mentioning his experiences in Dresden for the first time in print.
1967	Awarded Guggenheim Fellowship; travels to Dresden with Bernard V. O'Hare, who also survived the firestorm.
1968	*Welcome to the Monkey House* is published by Delacorte Press/Seymour Lawrence.
1969	*Slaughterhouse-Five* is published by Delacorte Press/Seymour Lawrence; it reaches number one on the *New York Times* Best Seller list.

1970 Travels to Biafra in January; begins to teach creative writing at Harvard University; *Happy Birthday, Wanda June* runs on and off Broadway for six months.

1971 Awarded an M.A. by the University of Chicago for *Cat's Cradle*; separates from Jane and moves to New York.

1972 On March 13, *Between Time and Timbuktu* airs on public television; elected a member of the National Institute of Arts and Letters and becomes Vice President of P.E.N. American Center.

1973 *Breakfast of Champions* is published by Delacorte Press/Seymour Lawrence; is awarded an LHD by Indiana University and becomes Distinguished Professor of English Prose at City University of New York.

1974 *Wampeters, Foma & Granfalloons*, a collection of speeches, essays, and interviews, is published by Delacorte Press/Seymour Lawrence; is awarded an honorary Litt.D. by Hobart and William Smith College; resigns position at City University of New York.

1975 Vice President of the National Institute of Arts and Letters; Mark Vonnegut's *Eden Express* is published.

1976 *Slapstick, or Lonesome No More!* is published by Delacorte Press/Seymour Lawrence.

1979 Marries Jill Krementz on November 24, whom he met first while working on *Happy Birthday, Wanda* June.

1979 *Jailbird* is published by Delacorte Press/Seymour Lawrence.

1980 Writes text for children's book, *Sun Moon Star*, from the illustrations of Ivan Chermayeff.

1981 *Palm Sunday: an Autobiographical Collage* is published by Delacorte Press.

1982 Lily Vonnegut is born; *Deadeye Dick* is published by Delacorte Press/Seymour Lawrence.

1985 *Galápagos* is published by Delacorte Press/Seymour Lawrence; attempts suicide.

1987   *Bluebeard* is published by Delacorte Press.

1990   *Hocus Pocus* is published by G.P. Putnam's Sons.

1991   *Fates Worse Than Death: An Autobiographical Collage of the 1980's* is published by G.P. Putnam's Sons.

1997   Brother Bernard Vonnegut dies; *Timequake* is published by G.P. Putnam's Sons.

1999   The film *Breakfast of Champions* is released; *Bagombo Snuff Box* is published by G.P. Putnam's Sons; *God Bless You, Dr. Kevorkian* is published by Seven Stories Press.

2000   Hospitalized for smoke inhalation after a house fire.

2000–2001   Teaches creative writing at Smith College, Northampton, Mass; named state author for New York.

Player Piano (1952)

The Sirens of Titan (1959)

Mother Night (1961)

Cat's Cradle (1963)

God Bless You, Mr. Rosewater (1965)

Welcome to the Monkey House (1968)

Slaughterhouse-Five (1969)

Happy Birthday, Wanda June: A Play (1971)

Between Time and Timbuktu: Or Prometheus-5, a Space Fantasy (1972)

Breakfast of Champions (1973)

Wampeters, Foma & Granfalloons (1974)

Slapstick (1976)

Jailbird (1979)

Palm Sunday (1981)

Deadeye Dick (1982)

Galapagos (1985)

Bluebeard (1987)

Hocus Pocus (1990)

Fates Worse Than Death (1991)

Timequake (1997)

Bagombo Snuff Box (1999)

God Bless You, Dr. Kevorkian (1999)

Abel, David. "So It Goes for Vonnegut at Smith, 78-Year-Old Author Still Shaking Up the Establishment." *The Boston Globe.* May 5, 2001: 1.

Allen, W.R., ed. *Conversations with Kurt Vonnegut.* Jackson: University Press of Mississippi, 1988.

———. *Understanding Kurt Vonnegut.* Columbia, South Carolina: University of South Carolina Press, 1991.

Anderson, Lisa. "Vonnegut's vision 'I had such high hopes for the planet ... after everyone had sacrificed so much and behaved so well'" *Chicago Tribune.* September 2, 1990: 1.

Bloom. Harold, ed. *Kurt Vonnegut.* Modern Critical Views. Philadelphia: Chelsea House Publishers, 2000.

———. *Kurt Vonnegut's Slaughterhouse-Five.* Modern Critical Interpretations. Philadelphia: Chelsea House Publishers, 2001.

———. *Kurt Vonnegut's Cat's Cradle. Modern Critical Interpretations.* Philadelphia: Chelsea House Publishers, 2002.

Bly, William. *Kurt Vonnegut's Slaughterhouse-Five.* Woodbury, NY: Barron's Educational Series, 1985.

Boon, Kevin A. *Chaos Theory and the Interpretation of Literary Texts: The Case of Kurt Vonnegut.* Lewiston, NY: Edwin Mellen Press, 1997.

———, ed. *At Millennium's End: New Essays on the Work of Kurt Vonnegut.* Albany, NY: State University of New York Press, 2001.

Broer, L.R. *Sanity Plea: Schizophrenia in the Novels of Kurt Vonnegut.* Tuscaloosa: University of Alabama Press, 1989.

Bryant, J.H. *The Open Decision: The Contemporary American Novel and Its Intellectual Background.* New York: Free Press, 1970.

Chernuchin, Michael, ed. *Vonnegut Talks!* Forest Hills, NY: Pylon Press, 1977.

Crichton, J. Michael. "Sci-Fi and Vonnegut." *The New Republic.* April 26, 1969: 33–35.

"The Devil's Work." *New York Times.* November 17, 1973.

Giannone, R. *Vonnegut: A Preface to His Novels.* Port Washington: Kennikat Press, 1977.

Goldsmith, David H. *Kurt Vonnegut: Fantasist of Fire and Ice.* Bowling Green, OH: Bowling Green University Popular Press, 1972.

Hassan, Ihab. *Liberations.* Middletown, Conn.: Wesleyan University Press 1971.

Hayman, D., D. Michaelis, et al. "The Art of Fiction LXIV." *The Paris Review* 69: 55–103, 1977.

Hicks, G. "Literary Horizons." *Saturday Review.* March 29, 1969: 25.

Hill, Gladwin. "Ten Cities Bombed" *New York Times.* February 15, 1945.

Klinkowitz, J. and J. Somer, eds. *The Vonnegut Statement.* New York: Delacorte Press, 1973.

Klinkowitz, J. and D.L. Lawler, eds. *Vonnegut in America : An Introduction to the Life and Work of Kurt Vonnegut.* New York: Delacorte Press, 1977.

Klinkowitz, J. *Kurt Vonnegut.* New York: Methuen & Co, 1982.

———. *Vonnegut in Fact: The Public Spokesmanship of Personal Fiction.* Columbia, South Carolina: University of South Carolina Press, 1998.

———. *The Vonnegut Effect.* Columbia, South Carolina: University of South Carolina Press, 2004.

Kramer, Carol. "Kurt's College Cult Adopts Him as Literary Guru at 48." *Chicago Tribune.* November 15, 1970.

Krim, S. "*Jailbird* Review." *The Village Voice.* New York: 81–82, 1979.

Leeds, Marc. *The Vonnegut Encyclopedia: An Authorized Compendium.* Westport, CT: Greenwood Publishing Group, 1995.

Leeds, Marc and Peter J. Reed. *Kurt Vonnegut: Images and Representations.* Westport, CT: Greenwood Publishing Group, 2000.

Lehmann-Haupt, Christopher. *Slaughterhouse-Five. New York Times* book review. March 31, 1969.

Leonard, J. "Black Magic." *The Nation.* 251: 421–425, 1990.

Levin, Martin "Do Human Beings Matter?: *God Bless You, Mr. Rosewater.* Or Pearls Before Swine." *New York Times* April 25, 1965.

Lundquist, J. *Kurt Vonnegut.* New York: Ungar, 1977.

Marvin, Thomas F. *Kurt Vonnegut: A Critical Companion.* Westport, CT: Greenwood Publishing Group, 2002.

Mayo, C. *Kurt Vonnegut : The Gospel from Outer Space : (or, Yes We Have No Nirvanas).* San Bernadino, California: Borgo Press, 1977.

Merrill, R., ed. *Critical Essays on Kurt Vonnegut.* Boston: G.K. Hall & Co, 1990.

Morse, Donald E. *Novels of Kurt Vonnegut: Imagining Being an American.* Westport, CT: Praeger Publishers, 2003.

Mustazza, Leonard. *Forever Pursuing Genesis: The Myth of Eden in the Novels of Kurt Vonnegut.* Lewisburg, PA: Bucknell University Press, 1990.

Rackstraw, Loree, ed. *Draftings in Vonnegut: The Paradox of Hope.* Cedar Falls, IA: University of Northern Iowa Press, 1988.

Reed, P.J. *Kurt Vonnegut, Jr.* New York: Thomas Y. Crowell Co, 1972.

———. *The Short Fiction of Kurt Vonnegut.* Westport, Conn.: Greenwood Press, 1997.

———. Kurt Vonnegut's Fantastic Faces. *Journal of the Fantastic in the Arts* 10, 1999.

Reed, P.J. and M. Leeds, eds. *The Vonnegut Chronicles: Interviews and Essays.* Contributions to the Study of World Literature. Westport, Connecticut: Greenwood Press, 1996.

Sale, Roger. "Kurt Vonnegut: writing with interchangeable parts." *New York Times.* October 3, 1976.

Sayers, Valerie. "Vonnegut Stew." *New York Times.* September 28, 1997.

Schatt, S. *Kurt Vonnegut, Jr.* Boston: Twayne Publishers, 1976.

Scholes, Robert. "Slapstick." Letter to the Editor. New York Times. November 21, 1976.

Seed, D. *Mankind Vs. Machines: The Technological Dystopia in Vonnegut's Player Piano.* Impossibility Fiction: Alternativity, Extrapolation, Speculation. D. Littlewood and P. Stockwell. Amsterdam ; Atlanta, GA: Rodopi. 17: 211, 1996.

Short, R. *Something to Believe In: Is Kurt Vonnegut the Exorcist or Jesus Christ Superstar?* San Francisco: Harper & Row, Publishers, 1978.

Streitfeld, David. "Vonnegut, From Cradle To Grave; The Writer and Failed Suicide, On the Fate of Survival. *The Washington Post.* August 29, 1991: c. 01.

Tanner, T. The Uncertain Messenger: A Study of the Novels of Kurt Vonnegut, Jr. *Critical Quarterly* 11:297–315, 1969.

Vonnegut, Kurt. "Speaking of Books: Science Fiction." *New York Times.* September 5, 1965.

———. *New York Times.* October 6, 1985.

———. Letter to the Editor. *New York Times.* March 27, 1991.

———. "Something's Rotten." *New York Times.* April 11, 1991.

———."Venture for Vonnegut: Visual art novelist, 73, got his start on vodka ad Article 1 of 2 found." *Denver Post.* September 14, 1996.

Vonnegut, Mark. *Eden Express.* New York: Praeger Publishers, Inc., 1975

Whitlark, J. *Vonnegut's Anthropology Thesis.* Literature and Anthropology. P. Dennis and W. Aycock. Lubbock: Texas Tech University Press, 1989.

Wright, Robert A. "Broad Spectrum of Writers Attacks Obscenity Ruling." *New York Times.* August 21, 1973.

Wood, Michael. "Vonnegut's Softer Focus." *New York Times* Review. September 9, 1979.

Yarmolinsky, Jane Vonnegut. *Angles Without Wings: A Courageous Family's Triumph over Tragedy.* Boston: Houghton Mifflin, 1987.

JOHN TOMEDI earned his B.A. in English from the Pennsylvania State University. He is a freelance writer and researcher living in Howard, Pennsylvania.

PETER J. REED is Professor Emeritus at the University of Minnesota and one of the foremost Vonnegut scholars in the academic world. His books include Kurt Vonnegut, Jr., The Short Fiction of Kurt Vonnegut, The Vonnegut Chronicles (with Marc Leeds), and Kurt Vonnegut: Images and Representations (with Marc Leeds).

B
VON

Tomedi, John. **8352**

Kurt Vonnegut